The Art of

The Art of Thought

This book includes two works by James Allen:

As a Man Thinketh
&
Master of Destiny

The Art of Thought is comprised of two books from James Allen: *As a Man Thinketh* and *Master of Destiny,* essential reading for those that want to unlock the true power of their mind and take control of their life.

Master of Destiny starts on page 52.

As a Man Thinketh

by
James Allen

Originally published in 1903

A man's mind may be likened to a garden, which may be intelligently cultivated or allowed to run wild; but whether cultivated or neglected, it must, and will, bring forth.

Table of contents

Chapter 1: *Thought and Character,* Page 7

Chapter 2: *Effect of Thought and Circumstances,* Page 12

Chapter 3: *Effect of Thought on Health* Page 28

Chapter 4: *Thought and Purpose,* Page 32

Chapter 5: *The Thought-Factor in Achievement,* Page 36

Chapter 6: *Visions and Ideals,* Page 41

Chapter 7: *Serenity,* Page 47

Foreword

This little volume (the result of meditation and experience) is not intended as an exhaustive treatise on the much-written-upon subject of the power of thought. It is suggestive rather than explanatory, its object being to stimulate men and women to the discovery and perception of the truth that—

"They themselves are makers of themselves"

by virtue of the thoughts which they choose and encourage; that mind is the master-weaver, both of the inner garment of character and the outer garment of circumstance, and that, as they may have hitherto woven in ignorance and pain they may now weave in enlightenment and happiness.

- James Allen

Thought and Character

"Man is made or unmade by himself; in the armory of thought he forges the weapons by which he destroys himself"

The aphorism, "As a man thinketh in his heart so is he," not only embraces the whole of a man's being, but is so comprehensive as to reach out to every condition and circumstance of his life. A man is literally what he thinks, his character being the complete sum of all his thoughts.

As the plant springs from, and could not be without, the seed, so every act of a man springs from the hidden seeds of thought, and could not have appeared without them. This applies equally to those acts called "spontaneous" and "unpremeditated" as to those which are deliberately executed.

Act is the blossom of thought, and joy and suffering are its fruits; thus does a man garner in the sweet and bitter fruitage of his own husbandry.

*"Thought in the mind hath made us, What we are
By thought was wrought and built. If a man's mind
Hath evil thoughts, pain comes on him as comes
The wheel the ox behind. . . .
. . If one endure
In purity of thought, joy follows him
As his own shadow—sure."*

Man is a growth by law, and not a creation by artifice, and cause and effect is as absolute and undeviating in the hidden realm of thought as in the world of visible and material things. A noble and Godlike character is not a thing of favor or chance, but is the natural result of continued effort in right thinking, the effect of long-cherished association with Godlike thoughts. An ignoble and bestial character, by the same process, is the result of the continued harboring of groveling thoughts.

Man is made or unmade by himself; in the armory of thought he forges the weapons by which he destroys himself; he also fashions the tools with which he builds for himself heavenly mansions of joy and strength and peace. By the right choice and true application of thought, man ascends to the Divine Perfection; by the abuse and wrong application of thought, he descends below the level of the beast. Between these two extremes are all the grades of character, and man is their maker and master.

Of all the beautiful truths pertaining to the soul which have been restored and brought to light in this age, none is more gladdening or fruitful of divine promise and confidence than this—that man is the master of thought, the moulder of character, and the maker and shaper of condition, environment, and destiny.

As a being of Power, Intelligence, and Love, and the lord of his own thoughts, man holds the key to every situation, and contains within himself that transforming and regenerative agency by which he may make himself what he wills.

Man is always the master, even in his weakest and most abandoned state; but in his weakness and degradation he is the foolish master who misgoverns his "household." When he begins to reflect upon his condition, and to search diligently for the Law upon which his being is established, he then becomes the wise master, directing his energies with intelligence, and fashioning his thoughts to fruitful issues. Such is the conscious master, and man can only thus become by discovering within himself the laws of thought; which discovery is totally a matter of application, self analysis, and experience.

Only by much searching and mining are gold and diamonds obtained, and man can find every truth connected with his being if he will dig deep into the mine of his soul; and that he is the maker of his character, the moulder of his life, and the builder of his destiny, he may unerringly prove, if he will watch, control, and alter his thoughts, tracing their effects upon himself, upon others, and upon his life and circumstances, linking cause and effect by patient practice and investigation, and utilizing his every experience, even to the most trivial, every-day occurrence, as a means of obtaining that knowledge of himself which is Understanding, Wisdom, Power. In this direction, as in no other, is the law absolute that "He that seeketh findeth; and to him that knocketh it shall be opened"; for only by patience, practice, and ceaseless importunity can a man enter the Door of the Temple of Knowledge.

Effect of Thought on Circumstances

"Every man is where he is by the law of his being; the thoughts which he has built into his character have brought him there"

A man's mind may be likened to a garden, which may be intelligently cultivated or allowed to run wild; but whether cultivated or neglected, it must, and will, bring forth. If no useful seeds are put into it, then an abundance of useless weed-seeds will fall therein, and will continue to produce their kind.

Just as a gardener cultivates his plot, keeping it free from weeds, and growing the flowers and fruits which he requires, so may a man tend the garden of his mind, weeding out all the wrong, useless, and impure thoughts, and cultivating toward perfection the flowers and fruits of right, useful, and pure thoughts. By pursuing this process, a man sooner or later discovers that he is the master-gardener of his soul, the director of his life. He also reveals, within himself, the laws of thought, and understands, with ever-increasing accuracy, how the thought-forces and mind-elements operate in the shaping of his character, circumstances, and destiny.

Thought and character are one, and as character can only manifest and discover itself through environment and circumstance, the outer conditions of a person's life will always be found to be harmoniously related to his inner state. This does not mean that a man's circumstances at any given time are an indication of his entire character, but that those circumstances are so intimately connected with some vital thought-element within himself that, for the time being, they are indispensable to his development.

Every man is where he is by the law of his being; the thoughts which he has built into his character have brought him there, and in the arrangement of his life there is no element of chance, but all is the result of a law which cannot err. This is just as true of those who feel "out of harmony" with their surroundings as of those who are contented with them.

As a progressive and evolving being, man is where he is that he may learn that he may grow; and as he learns the spiritual lesson which any circumstance contains for him, it passes away and gives place to other circumstances.

Man is buffeted by circumstances so long as he believes himself to be the creature of outside conditions, but when he realizes that he is a creative power, and that he may command the hidden soil and seeds of his being out of which circumstances grow, he then becomes the rightful master of himself.

That circumstances grow out of thought every man knows who has for any length of time practiced self-control and self-purification, for he will have noticed that the alteration in his circumstances has been in exact ratio with his altered mental condition. So true is this that when a man earnestly applies himself to remedy the defects in his character, and makes swift and marked progress, he passes rapidly through a succession of vicissitudes.

The soul attracts that which it secretly harbors; that which it loves, and also that which it fears; it reaches the height of its cherished aspirations; it falls to the level of its unchastened desires,—and circumstances are the means by which the soul receives its own.

Every thought-seed sown or allowed to fall into the mind, and to take root there, produces its own, blossoming sooner or later into act, and bearing its own fruitage of opportunity and circumstance. Good thoughts bear good fruit, bad thoughts bad fruit.

The outer world of circumstance shapes itself to the inner world of thought, and both pleasant and unpleasant external conditions are factors which make for the ultimate good of the individual. As the reaper of his own harvest, man learns both by suffering and bliss.

Following the inmost desires, aspirations, thoughts, by which he allows himself to be dominated (pursuing the will-o'-the-wisps of impure imaginings or steadfastly walking the highway of strong and high endeavor), a man at last arrives at their fruition and fulfillment in the outer conditions of his life. The laws of growth and adjustment everywhere obtains.

A man does not come to the almshouse or the jail by the tyranny of fate or circumstance, but by the pathway of groveling thoughts and base desires. Nor does a pure-minded man fall suddenly into crime by stress of any mere external force; the criminal thought had long been secretly fostered in the heart, and the hour of opportunity revealed its gathered power. Circumstance does not make the man; it reveals him to himself. No such conditions can exist as descending into vice and its attendant sufferings apart from vicious inclinations, or ascending into virtue and its pure happiness without the continued cultivation of virtuous aspirations; and man, therefore, as the lord and master of thought, is the maker of himself, the shaper and author of environment. Even at birth the soul comes to its own, and through every step of its earthly pilgrimage it attracts those combinations of conditions which reveal itself, which are the reflections of its own purity and impurity, its strength and weakness.

Men do not attract that which they want, but that which they are. Their whims, fancies, and ambitions are thwarted at every step, but their inmost thoughts and desires are fed with their own food, be it foul or clean. The "divinity that shapes our ends" is in ourselves; it is our very self. Man is manacled only by himself: thought and action are the jailers of Fate—they imprison, being base; they are also the angels of Freedom—they liberate, being noble. Not what he wishes and prays for does a man get, but what he justly earns. His wishes and prayers are only gratified and answered when they harmonize with his thoughts and actions.

In the light of this truth, what, then, is the meaning of "fighting against circumstances?" It means that a man is continually revolting against an effect without, while all the time he is nourishing and preserving its cause in his heart. That cause may take the form of a conscious vice or an unconscious weakness; but whatever it is, it stubbornly retards the efforts of its possessor, and thus calls aloud for remedy.

Men are anxious to improve their circumstances, but are unwilling to improve themselves; they therefore remain bound. The man who does not shrink from self-crucifixion can never fail to accomplish the object upon which his heart is set. This is as true of earthly as of heavenly things. Even the man whose sole object is to acquire wealth must be prepared to make great personal sacrifices before he can accomplish his object; and how much more so he who would realize a strong and well-poised life?

Here is a man who is wretchedly poor. He is extremely anxious that his surroundings and home comforts should be improved, yet all the time he shirks his work, and considers he is justified in trying to deceive his employer on the ground of the insufficiency of his wages. Such a man does not understand the simplest rudiments of those principles which are the basis of true prosperity, and is not only totally unfitted to rise out of his wretchedness, but is actually attracting to himself a still deeper wretchedness by dwelling in, and acting out, indolent, deceptive, and unmanly thoughts.

Here is a rich man who is the victim of a painful and persistent disease as the result of gluttony. He is willing to give large sums of money to get rid of it, but he will not sacrifice his gluttonous desires. He wants to gratify his taste for rich and unnatural viands and have his health as well. Such a man is totally unfit to have health, because he has not yet learned the first principles of a healthy life.

Here is an employer of labour who adopts crooked measures to avoid paying the regulation wage, and, in the hope of making larger profits, reduces the wages of his work-people. Such a man is altogether unfitted for prosperity, and when he finds himself bankrupt, both as regards reputation and riches, he blames circumstances, not knowing that he is the sole author of his condition.

I have introduced these three cases merely as illustrative of the truth that man is the causer (though nearly always unconsciously) of his circumstances, and that, whilst aiming at a good end, he is continually frustrating its accomplishment by encouraging thoughts and desires which cannot possibly harmonize with that end. Such cases could be multiplied and varied almost indefinitely, but this is not necessary, as the reader can, if he so resolves, trace the action of the laws of thought in his own mind and life, and until this is done, mere external facts cannot serve as a ground of reasoning.

Circumstances, however, are so complicated, thought is so deeply rooted, and the conditions of happiness vary so vastly with individuals, that a man's entire soul-condition (although it may be known to himself) cannot be judged by another from the external aspect of his life alone. A man may be honest in certain directions, yet suffer privations; a man may be dishonest in certain directions, yet acquire wealth; but the conclusion usually formed that the one man fails because of his particular honesty, and that the other prospers because of his particular dishonesty, is the result of a superficial judgment, which assumes that the dishonest man is almost totally corrupt, and the honest man almost entirely virtuous. In the light of a deeper knowledge and wider experience, such judgment is found to be erroneous. The dishonest man may have some admirable virtues which the other does, not possess; and the honest man obnoxious vices which are absent in the other. The honest man reaps the good results of his honest thoughts and acts; he also brings upon himself the sufferings, which his vices produce. The dishonest man likewise garners his own suffering and happiness.

It is pleasing to human vanity to believe that one suffers because of one's virtue; but not until a man has extirpated every sickly, bitter, and impure thought from his mind, and washed every sinful stain from his soul, can he be in a position to know and declare that his sufferings are the result of his good, and not of his bad qualities; and on the way to, yet long before he has reached, that supreme perfection, he will have found, working in his mind and life, the Great Law which is absolutely just, and which cannot, therefore, give good for evil, evil for good. Possessed of such knowledge, he will then know, looking back upon his past ignorance and blindness, that his life is, and always was, justly ordered, and that all his past experiences, good and bad, were the equitable outworking of his evolving, yet unevolved self.

Good thoughts and actions can never produce bad results; bad thoughts and actions can never produce good results. This is but saying that nothing can come from corn but corn, nothing from nettles but nettles. Men understand this law in the natural world, and work with it; but few understand it in the mental and moral world (though its operation there is just as simple and undeviating), and they, therefore, do not co-operate with it.

Suffering is always the effect of wrong thought in some direction. It is an indication that the individual is out of harmony with himself, with the Law of his being. The sole and supreme use of suffering is to purify, to burn out all that is useless and impure. Suffering ceases for him who is pure. There could be no object in burning gold after the dross had been removed, and a perfectly pure and enlightened being could not suffer.

The circumstances which a man encounters with suffering are the result of his own mental inharmony. The circumstances which a man encounters with blessedness, are the result of his own mental harmony. Blessedness not material possessions, is the measure of right thought; wretchedness, not lack of material possessions, is the measure of wrong thought. A man may be cursed and rich; he may be blessed and poor. Blessedness and riches are only joined together when the riches are rightly and wisely used; and the poor man only descends into wretchedness when he regards his lot as a burden unjustly imposed.

Indigence and indulgence are the two extremes of wretchedness. They are both equally unnatural and the result of mental disorder. A man is not rightly conditioned until he is a happy, healthy, and prosperous being; and happiness, health, and prosperity are the result of a harmonious adjustment of the inner with the outer, of the man with his surroundings.

A man only begins to be a man when he ceases to whine and revile, and commences to search for the hidden justice which regulates his life. And as he adapts his mind to that regulating factor, he ceases to accuse others as the cause of his condition, and builds himself up in strong and noble thoughts; ceases to kick against circumstances, but begins to use them as aids to his more rapid progress, and as a means of discovering the hidden powers and possibilities within himself.

Law, not confusion, is the dominating principle in the universe; justice, not injustice, is the soul and substance of life; and righteousness, not corruption, is the moulding and moving force in the spiritual government of the world. This being so, man has but to right himself to find that the universe is right; and during the process of putting himself right, he will find that as he alters his thoughts towards things and other people, things and other people will alter towards him.

The proof of this truth is in every person, and it therefore admits of easy investigation by systematic introspection and self-analysis. Let a man radically alter his thoughts, and he will be astonished at the rapid transformation it will effect in the material conditions of his life. Men imagine that thought can be kept secret, but it cannot; it rapidly crystallizes into habit, and habit solidifies into circumstance. Bestial thoughts crystallize into habits of drunkenness and sensuality, which solidify into circumstances of destitution and disease: impure thoughts of every kind crystallize into enervating and confusing habits, which solidify into distracting and adverse circumstances: thoughts of fear, doubt, and indecision crystallize into weak, unmanly, and irresolute habits, which solidify into circumstances of failure, indigence, and slavish dependence: lazy thoughts crystallize into habits of uncleanliness and dishonesty, which solidify into circumstances of foulness and beggary: hateful and condemnatory thoughts crystallize into habits of accusation and violence, which solidify into circumstances of injury and persecution: selfish thoughts of all kinds crystallize into habits of self-seeking, which solidify into circumstances more or less distressing. On the other hand, beautiful thoughts of all kinds crystallize into habits of grace and kindliness, which solidify into genial and sunny circumstances: pure thoughts crystallize into habits of temperance and self-control, which solidify into circumstances of repose and peace: thoughts of courage, self-reliance, and decision crystallize into manly habits, which solidify into circumstances of success, plenty, and freedom: energetic thoughts crystallize into habits of cleanliness and industry, which solidify into circumstances of pleasantness: gentle and forgiving thoughts crystallize into habits of gentleness, which solidify into protective and preservative circumstances: loving and unselfish thoughts crystallize into habits of self-forgetfulness for others, which solidify into circumstances of sure and abiding prosperity and true riches.

A particular train of thought persisted in, be it good or bad, cannot fail to produce its results on the character and circumstances. A man cannot directly choose his circumstances, but he can choose his thoughts, and so indirectly, yet surely, shape his circumstances.

Nature helps every man to the gratification of the thoughts which he most encourages, and opportunities are presented which will most speedily bring to the surface both the good and evil thoughts.

Let a man cease from his sinful thoughts, and all the world will soften towards him, and be ready to help him; let him put away his weakly and sickly thoughts, and lo! opportunities will spring up on every hand to aid his strong resolves; let him encourage good thoughts, and no hard fate shall bind him down to wretchedness and shame. The world is your kaleidoscope, and the varying combinations of colors which at every succeeding moment it presents to you are the exquisitely adjusted pictures of your ever-moving thoughts.

> *You will be what you will to be;*
> *Let failure find its false content*
> *In that poor word, 'environment,'*
> *But spirit scorns it, and is free.*

"It masters time, it conquers space;
It cows that boastful trickster, Chance,
And bids the tyrant Circumstance
Uncrown, and fill a servant's place.
"The human Will, that force unseen,
The offspring of a deathless Soul,
Can hew a way to any goal,
Though walls of granite intervene.
"Be not impatient in delay,
But wait as one who understands;
When spirit rises and commands,
The gods are ready to obey.

Effect of Thought on Health and The Body

"Change of diet will not help a man who will not change his thoughts. When a man makes his thoughts pure, he no longer desires impure food"

The body is the servant of the mind. It obeys the operations of the mind, whether they be deliberately chosen or automatically expressed. At the bidding of unlawful thoughts the body sinks rapidly into disease and decay; at the command of glad and beautiful thoughts it becomes clothed with youthfulness and beauty.

Disease and health, like circumstances, are rooted in thought. Sickly thoughts will express themselves through a sickly body. Thoughts of fear have been known to kill a man as speedily as a bullet, and they are continually killing thousands of people just as surely though less rapidly. The people who live in fear of disease are the people who get it. Anxiety quickly demoralizes the whole body, and lays it open to the entrance of disease; while impure thoughts, even if not physically indulged, will soon shatter the nervous system.

Strong, pure, and happy thoughts build up the body in vigor and grace. The body is a delicate and plastic instrument, which responds readily to the thoughts by which it is impressed, and habits of thought will produce their own effects, good or bad, upon it.

Men will continue to have impure and poisoned blood so long as they propagate unclean thoughts. Out of a clean heart comes a clean life and a clean body. Out of a defiled mind proceeds a defiled life and a corrupt body. Thought is the fount of action, life, and manifestation; make the fountain pure, and all will be pure.

Change of diet will not help a man who will not change his thoughts. When a man makes his thoughts pure, he no longer desires impure food.

Clean thoughts make clean habits. The so-called saint who does not wash his body is not a saint. He who has strengthened and purified his thoughts does not need to consider the malevolent microbe.

If you would perfect your body, guard your mind. If you would renew your body, beautify your mind. Thoughts of malice, envy, disappointment, despondency, rob the body of its health and grace. A sour face does not come by chance; it is made by sour thoughts. Wrinkles that mar are drawn by folly, passion, pride.

I know a woman of ninety-six who has the bright, innocent face of a girl. I know a man well under middle age whose face is drawn into inharmonious contours. The one is the result of a sweet and sunny disposition; the other is the outcome of passion and discontent.

As you cannot have a sweet and wholesome abode unless you admit the air and sunshine freely into your rooms, so a strong body and a bright, happy, or serene countenance can only result from the free admittance into the mind of thoughts of joy and goodwill and serenity.

On the faces of the aged there are wrinkles made by sympathy; others by strong and pure thought, and others are carved by passion: who cannot distinguish them? With those who have lived righteously, age is calm, peaceful, and softly mellowed, like the setting sun. I have recently seen a philosopher on his death-bed. He was not old except in years. He died as sweetly and peacefully as he had lived.

There is no physician like cheerful thought for dissipating the ills of the body; there is no comforter to compare with goodwill for dispersing the shadows of grief and sorrow. To live continually in thoughts of ill-will, cynicism, suspicion, and envy, is to be confined in a self-made prison. But to think well of all, to be cheerful with all, to patiently learn to find the good in all —such unselfish thoughts are the very portals of heaven; and to dwell day by day in thoughts of peace toward every creature will bring abounding peace to their possessor.

Thought and Purpose

"He who has conquered doubt and fear has conquered failure"

Until thought is linked with purpose there is no intelligent accomplishment. With the majority the barque of thought is allowed to "drift" upon the ocean of life. Aimlessness is a vice, and such drifting must not continue for him who would steer clear of catastrophe and destruction.

They who have no central purpose in their life fall an easy prey to petty worries, fears, troubles, and self-pityings, all of which are indications of weakness, which lead, just as surely as deliberately planned sins (though by a different route), to failure, unhappiness, and loss, for weakness cannot persist in a power-evolving universe.

A man should conceive of a legitimate purpose in his heart, and set out to accomplish it. He should make this purpose the centralizing point of his thoughts. It may take the form of a spiritual ideal, or it may be a worldly object, according to his nature at the time being; but whichever it is, he should steadily focus his thought-forces upon the object which he has set before him. He should make this purpose his supreme duty, and should devote himself to its attainment, not allowing his thoughts to wander away into ephemeral fancies, longings, and imaginings. This is the royal road to self-control and true concentration of thought. Even if he fails again and again to accomplish his purpose (as he necessarily must until weakness is overcome), the strength of character gained will be the measure of his true success, and this will form a new starting-point for future power and triumph.

Those who are not prepared for the apprehension of a great purpose, should fix the thoughts upon the faultless performance of their duty, no matter how insignificant their task may appear. Only in this way can the thoughts be gathered and focussed, and resolution and energy be developed, which being done, there is nothing which may not be accomplished.

The weakest soul, knowing its own weakness, and believing this truth—that strength can only be developed by effort and practice, will, thus believing, at once begin to exert itself, and, adding effort to effort, patience to patience, and strength to strength, will never cease to develop, and will at last grow divinely strong.

As the physically weak man can make himself strong by careful and patient training, so the man of weak thoughts can make them strong by exercising himself in right thinking.

To put away aimlessness and weakness, and to begin to think with purpose, is to enter the ranks of those strong ones who only recognize failure as one of the pathways to attainment; who make all conditions serve them, and who think strongly, attempt fearlessly, and accomplish masterfully.

Having conceived of his purpose, a man should mentally mark out a straight pathway to its achievement, looking neither to the right nor the left. Doubts and fears should be rigorously excluded; they are disintegrating elements which break up the straight line of effort, rendering it crooked, ineffectual, useless. Thoughts of doubt and fear never accomplish anything, and never can. They always lead to failure. Purpose, energy, power to do, and all strong thoughts cease when doubt and fear creep in.

The will to do springs from the knowledge that we can do. Doubt and fear are the great enemies of knowledge, and he who encourages them, who does not slay them, thwarts himself at every step.

He who has conquered doubt and fear has conquered failure. His every thought is allied with power, and all difficulties are bravely met and wisely overcome. His purposes are seasonably planted, and they bloom and bring forth fruit which does not fall prematurely to the ground.

Thought allied fearlessly to purpose becomes creative force: he who knows this is ready to become something higher and stronger than a mere bundle of wavering thoughts and fluctuating sensations; he who does this has become the conscious and intelligent wielder of his mental powers.

The Thought-Factor in Achievement

"A man can only rise, conquer, and achieve by lifting up his thoughts."

All that a man achieves and all that he fails to achieve is the direct result of his own thoughts. In a justly ordered universe, where loss of equipoise would mean total destruction, individual responsibility must be absolute. A man's weakness and strength, purity and impurity, are his own, and not another man's; they are brought about by himself, and not by another; and they can only be altered by himself, never by another. His condition is also his own, and not another man's. His suffering and his happiness are evolved from within. As he thinks, so he is; as he continues to think, so he remains.

A strong man cannot help a weaker unless that weaker is willing to be helped, and even then the weak man must become strong of himself; he must, by his own efforts, develop the strength which he admires in another. None but himself can alter his condition.

It has been usual for men to think and to say, "Many men are slaves because one is an oppressor; let us hate the oppressor." Now, however, there is amongst an increasing few a tendency to reverse this judgment, and to say, "One man is an oppressor because many are slaves; let us despise the slaves." The truth is that oppressor and slave are co-operators in ignorance, and, while seeming to afflict each other, are in reality afflicting themselves. A perfect Knowledge perceives the action of law in the weakness of the oppressed and the misapplied power of the oppressor; a perfect Love, seeing the suffering which both states entail, condemns neither; a perfect Compassion embraces both oppressor and oppressed.

He who has conquered weakness, and has put away all selfish thoughts, belongs neither to oppressor nor oppressed. He is free.

A man can only rise, conquer, and achieve by lifting up his thoughts. He can only remain weak, and abject, and miserable by refusing to lift up his thoughts.

Before a man can achieve anything, even in worldly things, he must lift his thoughts above slavish animal indulgence. He may not, in order to succeed, give up all animality and selfishness, by any means; but a portion of it must, at least, be sacrificed. A man whose first thought is bestial indulgence could neither think clearly nor plan methodically; he could not find and develop his latent resources, and would fail in any undertaking. Not having commenced manfully to control his thoughts, he is not in a position to control affairs and to adopt serious responsibilities. He is not fit to act independently and stand alone. But he is limited only by the thoughts which he chooses.

There can be no progress, no achievement without sacrifice, and a man's worldly success will be in the measure that he sacrifices his confused animal thoughts, and fixes his mind on the development of his plans, and the strengthening of his resolution and self-reliance. And the higher he lifts his thoughts, the more manly, upright, and righteous he becomes, the greater will be his success, the more blessed and enduring will be his achievements.

The universe does not favor the greedy, the dishonest, the vicious, although on the mere surface it may sometimes appear to do so; it helps the honest, the magnanimous, the virtuous. All the great Teachers of the ages have declared this in varying forms, and to prove and know it a man has but to persist in making himself more and more virtuous by lifting up his thoughts.

Intellectual achievements are the result of thought consecrated to the search for knowledge, or for the beautiful and true in life and nature. Such achievements may be sometimes connected with vanity and ambition, but they are not the outcome of those characteristics; they are the natural outgrowth of long and arduous effort, and of pure and unselfish thoughts.

Spiritual achievements are the consummation of holy aspirations. He who lives constantly in the conception of noble and lofty thoughts, who dwells upon all that is pure and unselfish, will, as surely as the sun reaches its zenith and the moon its full, become wise and noble in character, and rise into a position of influence and blessedness.

Achievement, of whatever kind, is the crown of effort, the diadem of thought. By the aid of self-control, resolution, purity, righteousness, and well-directed thought a man ascends; by the aid of animality, indolence, impurity, corruption, and confusion of thought a man descends.

A man may rise to high success in the world, and even to lofty altitudes in the spiritual realm, and again descend into weakness and wretchedness by allowing arrogant, selfish, and corrupt thoughts to take possession of him.

Victories attained by right thought can only be maintained by watchfulness. Many give way when success is assured, and rapidly fall back into failure.

All achievements, whether in the business, intellectual, or spiritual world, are the result of definitely directed thought, are governed by the same law and are of the same method; the only difference lies in the object of attainment.

He who would accomplish little must sacrifice little; he who would achieve much must sacrifice much; he who would attain highly must sacrifice greatly.

Visions and Ideals

"The Vision that you glorify in your mind, the Ideal that you enthrone in your heart—this you will build your life by, this you will become."

The dreamers are the saviors of the world. As the visible world is sustained by the invisible, so men, through all their trials and sins and sordid vocations, are nourished by the beautiful visions of their solitary dreamers. Humanity cannot forget its dreamers; it cannot let their ideals fade and die; it lives in them; it knows them as the realities which it shall one day see and know.

Composer, sculptor, painter, poet, prophet, sage, these are the makers of the after-world, the architects of heaven. The world is beautiful because they have lived; without them, laboring humanity would perish.

He who cherishes a beautiful vision, a lofty ideal in his heart, will one day realize it. Columbus cherished a vision of another world, and he discovered it; Copernicus fostered the vision of a multiplicity of worlds and a wider universe, and he revealed it; Buddha beheld the vision of a spiritual world of stainless beauty and perfect peace, and he entered into it.

Cherish your visions; cherish your ideals; cherish the music that stirs in your heart, the beauty that forms in your mind, the loveliness that drapes your purest thoughts, for out of them will grow all delightful conditions, all heavenly environment; of these, if you but remain true to them, your world will at last be built.

To desire is to obtain; to aspire is to achieve. Shall man's basest desires receive the fullest measure of gratification, and his purest aspirations starve for lack of sustenance? Such is not the Law: such a condition of things can never obtain: "Ask and receive."

Dream lofty dreams, and as you dream, so shall you become. Your Vision is the promise of what you shall one day be; your Ideal is the prophecy of what you shall at last unveil.

The greatest achievement was at first and for a time a dream. The oak sleeps in the acorn; the bird waits in the egg; and in the highest vision of the soul a waking angel stirs. Dreams are the seedlings of realities.

Your circumstances may be uncongenial, but they shall not long remain so if you but perceive an Ideal and strive to reach it. You cannot travel within and stand still without. Here is a youth hard pressed by poverty and labour; confined long hours in an unhealthy workshop; unschooled, and lacking all the arts of refinement. But he dreams of better things; he thinks of intelligence, of refinement, of grace and beauty. He conceives of, mentally builds up, an ideal condition of life; the vision of a wider liberty and a larger scope takes possession of him; unrest urges him to action, and he utilizes all his spare time and means, small though they are, to the development of his latent powers and resources. Very soon so altered has his mind become that the workshop can no longer hold him. It has become so out of harmony with his mentality that it falls out of his life as a garment is cast aside, and, with the growth of opportunities which fit the scope of his expanding powers, he passes out of it forever. Years later we see this youth as a full-grown man. We find him a master of certain forces of the mind which he wields with world-wide influence and almost unequalled power. In his hands he holds the cords of gigantic responsibilities; he speaks, and lo! lives are changed; men and women hang upon his words and remould their characters, and, sunlike, he becomes the fixed and luminous centre round which innumerable destinies revolve. He has realized the Vision of his youth. He has become one with his Ideal.

And you, too, youthful reader, will realize the Vision (not the idle wish) of your heart, be it base or beautiful, or a mixture of both, for you will always gravitate toward that which you, secretly, most love. Into your hands will be placed the exact results of your own thoughts; you will receive that which you earn; no more, no less. Whatever your present environment may be, you will fall, remain, or rise with your thoughts, your Vision, your Ideal. You will become as small as your controlling desire; as great as your dominant aspiration: in the beautiful words of Stanton Kirkham Davis, "You may be keeping accounts, and presently you shall walk out of the door that for so long has seemed to you the barrier of your ideals, and shall find yourself before an audience—the pen still behind your ear, the ink-stains on your fingers—and then and there shall pour out the torrent of your inspiration. You may be driving sheep, and you shall wander to the city—bucolic and open-mouthed; shall wander under the intrepid guidance of the spirit into the studio of the master, and after a time he shall say, 'I have nothing more to teach you.' And now you have become the master, who did so recently dream of great things while driving sheep. You shall lay down the saw and the plane to take upon yourself the regeneration of the world."

The thoughtless, the ignorant, and the indolent, seeing only the apparent effects of things and not the things themselves, talk of luck, of fortune, and chance. Seeing a man grow rich, they say, "How lucky he is!" Observing another become intellectual, they exclaim, "How highly favored he is!" And noting the saintly character and wide influence of another, they remark, "How chance aids him at every turn!" They do not see the trials and failures and struggles which these men have voluntarily encountered in order to gain their experience; have no knowledge of the sacrifices they have made, of the undaunted efforts they have put forth, of the faith they have exercised, that they might overcome the apparently insurmountable, and realize the Vision of their heart. They do not know the darkness and the heartaches; they only see the light and joy, and call it "luck"; do not see the long and arduous journey, but only behold the pleasant goal, and call it "good fortune"; do not understand the process, but only perceive the result, and call it "chance."

In all human affairs there are efforts, and there are results, and the strength of the effort is the measure of the result. Chance is not. "Gifts," powers, material, intellectual, and spiritual possessions are the fruits of effort; they are thoughts completed, objects accomplished, visions realized.

The Vision that you glorify in your mind, the Ideal that you enthrone in your heart—this you will build your life by, this you will become.

Serenity

"The more tranquil a man becomes, the greater is his success, his influence, his power for good"

Calmness of mind is one of the beautiful jewels of wisdom. It is the result of long and patient effort in self-control. Its presence is an indication of ripened experience, and of a more than ordinary knowledge of the laws and operations of thought.

A man becomes calm in the measure that he understands himself as a thought evolved being, for such knowledge necessitates the understanding of others as the result of thought, and as he develops a right understanding, and sees more and more clearly the internal relations of things by the action of cause and effect, he ceases to fuss and fume and worry and grieve, and remains poised, steadfast, serene.

The calm man, having learned how to govern himself, knows how to adapt himself to others; and they, in turn, reverence his spiritual strength, and feel that they can learn of him and rely upon him. The more tranquil a man becomes, the greater is his success, his influence, his power for good. Even the ordinary trader will find his business prosperity increase as he develops a greater self-control and equanimity, for people will always prefer to deal with a man whose demeanor is strongly equable.

The strong, calm man is always loved and revered. He is like a shade-giving tree in a thirsty land, or a sheltering rock in a storm. "Who does not love a tranquil heart, a sweet-tempered, balanced life? It does not matter whether it rains or shines, or what changes come to those possessing these blessings, for they are always sweet, serene, and calm. That exquisite poise of character which we call serenity is the last lesson of culture; it is the flowering of life, the fruitage of the soul. It is precious as wisdom, more to be desired than gold—yea, than even fine gold. How insignificant mere money seeking looks in comparison with a serene life—a life that dwells in the ocean of Truth, beneath the waves, beyond the reach of tempests, in the Eternal Calm!

"How many people we know who sour their lives, who ruin all that is sweet and beautiful by explosive tempers, who destroy their poise of character, and make bad blood! It is a question whether the great majority of people do not ruin their lives and mar their happiness by lack of self-control. How few people we meet in life who are well balanced, who have that exquisite poise which is characteristic of the finished character!"

Yes, humanity surges with uncontrolled passion, is tumultuous with ungoverned grief, is blown about by anxiety and doubt. Only the wise man, only he whose thoughts are controlled and purified, makes the winds and the storms of the soul obey him.

Tempest-tossed souls, wherever ye may be, under whatsoever conditions ye may live, know this—in the ocean of life the isles of Blessedness are smiling, and the sunny shore of your ideal awaits your coming. Keep your hand firmly upon the helm of thought. In the barque of your soul reclines the commanding Master; He does but sleep: wake Him. Self-control is strength;

Right Thought is mastery; Calmness is power. Say unto your heart, "Peace, be still!"

As a Man Thinketh

Master of Destiny

By
James Allen

Without strength of mind, nothing worthy of accomplishment can be done, and the cultivation of that steadfastness and stability of character which is commonly called "willpower" is one of the foremost duties of man, for its possession is essentially necessary both to his temporal and eternal well being.

Table of contents

Chapter 1: *Deeds, Character, and Destiny,* Page 57

Chapter 2: *The Science of Self-Control,* Page 69

Chapter 3: *Cause and Effect in Human Conduct,* Page 82

Chapter 4: *Training of the Will,* Page 90

Chapter 5: *Thoroughness,* Page 97

Chapter 6: *Mind-Building and Life-Building,* Page 103

Chapter 7: *Cultivation and Concentration,* Page 112

Chapter 8: *Practice of Meditation,* Page 124

Chapter 9: *The Power of Purpose,* Page 135

Chapter 10: *The Joy of Accomplishment,* Page 139

Prologue

The discovery of the law of Evolution in the material world has prepared men for a knowledge of the law of cause and effect in the mental world. Thought is not less orderly and progressive than the material forms which embody thought; and not alone cells and atoms, but thoughts and deeds are charged with a cumulative and selective energy. In the realm of thought and deed, the good survives, for it is the "fittest"; the evil ultimately perishes. To know that the "perfect law" of Causation is all embracing in mind as in matter, is to be relieved from all anxiety concerning the ultimate destiny of individuals and of humanity —

"For man is man and master of his fate" —

And the will in man which is conquering the knowledge of the natural law will conquer the knowledge of the spiritual law. The will which, in ignorance, chooses evil, will, as wisdom evolves and emerges, choose, good. In a universe of law, the final mastery of evil by man is assured. His lesser destinies of separation and sorrow, defeat and death, are but disciplinary steps leading to the Great Destiny of triumphant mastery. He himself is unconsciously building, albeit with lacerated hands and labour-bowed form, the Temple of Glory which is to afford him an eternal habitation of peace.

In this volume, I have tried to set down some words indicative of this Law and this Destiny and the manner of its working and its building; and have arranged the subject matter as to make the book a companion volume to the Life Triumphant. The first six, and the last chapters first appeared in the Bibby's Quarterly and the Bibby's Annual and it is by kind permission of the Editor Mr. Joseph Bibby, that they are now brought together and published in volume form, the other three chapters having been added to make the book consecutive and complete.

- James Allen

Master of Destiny

1
Deeds, Character, and Destiny

"Character is destiny itself; as a fixed combination of deeds, it bears within itself the results of those deeds"

THERE IS, and always has been, a widespread belief in Fate, or Destiny, that is, in an eternal and inscrutable Power which apportions definite ends to both individuals and nations. This belief has arisen from long observation of the facts of life. Men are conscious that there are certain occurrences which they cannot control, and are powerless to avert. Birth and death, for instance, are inevitable, and many of the incidents of life appear equally inevitable.

Men strain every nerve for the attainment of certain ends, and gradually they become conscious of a Power which seems to be not of themselves, which frustrates their puny efforts, and laughs, as it were, at their fruitless striving and struggle. As men advance in life, they learn to submit, more or less, to this overruling Power which they do not understand, perceiving only its effects in themselves and the world around them, and they call it by various names, such as God, Providence, Fate, Destiny, etc.

Men of contemplation, such as poets and philosophers, step aside, as it were, to watch the movements of this mysterious Power as it seems to elevate its favorites on the one hand, and strike down its victims on the other, without reference to merit or demerit.

The greatest poets, especially the dramatic poets, represent this Power in their works, as they have observed it in Nature. The Greek and Roman dramatists usually depict their heroes as having foreknowledge of their fate, and taking means to escape it; but by so doing they blindly involve themselves in a series of consequences which bring about the doom which they are trying to avert.

Shakespeare's characters, on the other hand, are represented, as in Nature, with no foreknowledge (except in the form of presentiment) of their particular destiny. Thus, according to the poets, whether the man knows his fate or not, he cannot avert it, and every conscious or unconscious act of his is a step towards it. Omar Khayyam's Moving Finger is a vivid expression of this idea of Fate:

"The Moving Finger writes, and having writ, Moves on: nor all thy Piety nor Wit Shall lure it back to cancel half a line, Nor all thy Tears wash out a Word of it."

Thus, men in all nations and times have experienced in their lives the action of this invincible Power or Law, and in our nation today this experience has been crystallized in the terse proverb, "Man proposes, God disposes." But, contradictory as it may appear, there is an equally widespread belief in man's responsibility as a free agent.

All moral teaching is an affirmation of man's freedom to choose his course and mold his destiny: and man's patient and untiring efforts in achieving his ends are declarations of consciousness of freedom and power.

This dual experience of fate on the one hand, and freedom on the other, has given rise to the interminable controversy between the believers in Fatalism and the upholders of free will -a controversy which was recently revived under the term "Determinism versus Freewill."

Between apparently conflicting extremes there is always a "middle way" of balance, justice, or compensation which, while it includes both extremes, cannot be said to be either one or the other, and which brings both into harmony; and this middle way is the point of contact between two extremes.

Truth cannot be a partisan, but, by its nature, is the Reconciler of extremes; and so, in the matter which we are considering, there is a "golden mean" which brings Fate and Free will into close relationship, wherein, indeed, it is seen that these two indisputable facts in human life, for such they are, are but two aspects of one central law, one unifying and all-embracing principle, namely, the law of causation in its moral aspect.

Moral causation necessitates both Fate and Free will, both individual responsibility and individual predestination, for the law of causes must also be the law of effects, and cause and effect must always be equal; the train of causation, both in matter and mind, must be eternally balanced, therefore eternally, just, eternally perfect.

Thus every effect may be said to be a thing preordained, but the predetermining power is a cause, and not the fiat of an arbitrary will. Man finds himself involved in the train of causation. His life is made up of causes and effects. It is both a sowing and a reaping. Each act of his is a cause which must be balanced by its effects. He chooses the cause (this is Free will), he cannot choose, alter, or avert the effect (this is Fate); thus Free will stands for the power to initiate causes, and destiny is involvement in effects.

It is therefore true that man is predestined to certain ends, but he himself has (though he knows it not) issued the mandate; that good or evil thing from which there is no escape, he has, by his own deeds, brought about. It may here be urged that man is not responsible for his deeds, that these are the effects of his character, and that he is not responsible for the character, good or bad, which was given him at his birth.

If character was "given him" at birth, this would be true, and there would then be no moral law, and no need for moral teaching; but characters are not given ready made, they are evolved; they are, indeed, effects, the products of the moral law itself, that is - the products of deeds. Character results of an accumulation of deeds which have been piled up, so to speak, by the individual during his life.

Man is the doer of his own deeds; as such he is the maker of his own character; and as the doer of his deeds and the maker of his character, he is the molder and shaper of his destiny. He has the power to modify and alter his deeds, and every time he acts he modifies his character, and with the modification of his character for good or evil, he is predetermining for himself new destinies - destinies disastrous or beneficent in accordance with the nature of his deeds.

Character is destiny itself; as a fixed combination of deeds, it bears within itself the results of those deeds. These results lie hidden as moral seeds in the dark recesses of the character, awaiting their season of germination, growth, and fruitage.

Those things which befall a man are the reflections of himself; that destiny which pursued him, which he was powerless to escape by effort, or avert by prayer, was the relentless ghoul of his own wrong deeds demanding and enforcing restitution; those blessings and curses which come to him unbidden are the reverberating echoes of the sounds which he himself sent forth.

It is this knowledge of the Perfect Law working through and above all things; of the Perfect Justice operating in and adjusting all human affairs, that enables the good man to love his enemies, and to rise above all hatred, resentment, and complaining; for he knows that only his own can come to him, and that, though he be surrounded by persecutors, his enemies are but the blind instruments of a faultless retribution; and so be blames them not, but calmly receives his accounts, and patiently pays his moral debts.

But this is not all; he does not merely pay his debts; be takes care not to contract any further debts. He watches himself and makes his deeds faultless. While paying off evil accounts, be is laying up good accounts. By putting an end to his own sin, he is bringing evil and suffering to an end.

And now let us consider how the Law operates in particular instances in the outworking of destiny through deeds and character. First, we will look at this present life, for the present is the synthesis of the entire past; the net result of all that a man has ever thought and done is contained within him.

It is noticeable that sometimes the good man fails and the unscrupulous man prospers - a fact which seems to put all moral maxims as to the good results of righteousness out of account - and because of this, many people deny the operation of any just law in human life, and even declare that it is chiefly the unjust that prosper.

Nevertheless, the moral law exists, and is not altered or subverted by shallow conclusions. It should be remembered that man is a changing, evolving being. The good man was not always good; the bad man was not always bad. Even in this life, there was a time, in a large number of instances, when the man who is now just, was unjust; when he who is now kind, was cruel; when he who is now pure, was impure.

Conversely, there was a time in this life, in a number of instances, when he who is now unjust, was just; when he who is now cruel, was kind; when he who is now impure, was pure. Thus, the good man who is overtaken with calamity today is reaping the result of his former evil sowing; later he will reap the happy result of his present good sowing; while the bad man is now reaping the result of his former good sowing; later he will reap the result of his present sowing of bad.

Characteristics are fixed habits of mind, the results of deeds. An act repeated a large number of times becomes unconscious, or automatic - that is, it then seems to repeat itself without any effort on the part of the doer, so that it seems to him almost impossible not to do it, and then it has become a mental characteristic.

Here is a poor man out of work. He is honest, and is not a shirker. He wants work, and cannot get it. He tries hard, and continues to fail. Where is the justice in his lot? There was a time in this man's condition when he had plenty of work. He felt burdened with it; he shirked it, and longed for ease. He thought how delightful it would be to have nothing to do. He did not appreciate the blessedness of his lot. His desire for ease is now gratified, but the fruit for which he longed, and which he thought would taste so sweet, has turned to ashes in his mouth. The condition which he aimed for, namely, to have nothing to do, he has reached, and there he is compelled to remain till his lesson is thoroughly learned. And he is surely learning that habitual ease is degrading, that to have nothing to do is a condition of wretchedness, and that work is a noble and blessed thing. His former desires and deeds have brought him where he is; and now his present desire for work, his ceaseless searching and asking for it, will just as surely bring about its own beneficent result. No longer desiring idleness, his present condition will, as an effect, the cause of which is no longer propagated, soon pass away, and he will obtain employment; and if his whole mind is now set on work, and he desires it above all else, then when it comes he will be overwhelmed with it; it will flow in to him from all sides, and he will prosper in his industry. Then, if he does not understand the law of cause and effect in human life, he will wonder why work comes to him apparently unsought, while others who seek it strenuously fail to obtain it. Nothing comes unbidden; where the shadow is, there also is the substance.

That which comes to the individual is the product of his own deeds. As cheerful industry leads to greater industry and increasing prosperity, and labor shirked or undertaken discontentedly leads to a lesser degree of labor and decreasing prosperity, so with all the varied conditions of life as we see them - they are the destinies wrought by the thoughts and deeds of each particular individual. So also with the vast variety of characters - they are the ripening and ripened growth of the sowing of deeds.

As the individual reaps what he sows, so the nation, being a community of individuals, reaps also what it sows. Nations become great when their leaders are just men; they fall and fade when their just men pass away. Those who are in power set an example, good or bad, for the entire nation. Great will be the peace and prosperity of a nation when there shall arise within it a line of statesmen who, having first established themselves in a lofty integrity of character, shall direct the energies of the nation toward the culture of virtue and development of character, knowing that only through personal industry, integrity, and nobility can national prosperity proceed. Still, above all, is the Great Law, calmly and with infallible justice meting out to mortals their fleeting destinies, tearstained or smiling, the fabric of their hands. Life is a great school for the development of character, and all, through strife and struggle, vice and virtue, success and failure, are slowly but surely learning the lessons of wisdom.

2
The Science of Self-Control

"He who understands and dominates the forces of external nature is the natural scientist; but be who understands and dominates the internal forces of the mind is the divine scientist"

WE LIVE in a scientific age. Men of science are numbered by thousands, and they are ceaselessly searching, analyzing, and experimenting with a view to discovery and the increase of knowledge. The shelves of our libraries, both public and private, are heavy with their load of imposing volumes on scientific subjects, and the wonderful achievements of modern science are always before us - whether in our homes or in our streets, in country or town, on land or sea - there shall we have before us some marvelous device, some recent accomplishment of science, for adding to our comfort, increasing our speed, or saving the labor of our hands.

Yet, with all our vast store of scientific knowledge, and its startling and rapidly increasing results in the world of discovery and invention, there is, in this age, one branch of science which has so far fallen into decay as to have become almost forgotten; a science, nevertheless, which is of greater importance than all the other sciences combined, and without which all science would but subserve the ends of selfishness, and aid in man's destruction - I refer to the Science of Self-control.

Our modern scientists study the elements and forces which are outside themselves, with the object of controlling and utilizing them. The ancients studied the elements and forces which were within themselves, with a view to controlling and utilizing them, and the ancients produced such mighty Masters of knowledge in this direction, that to this day they are held in reverence as gods, and the vast religious organizations of the world are based upon their achievements.

Wonderful as are the forces in nature, they are vastly inferior to that combination of intelligent forces which comprise the mind of man, and which dominate and direct the blind mechanical forces of nature. Therefore, it follows that, to understand, control, and direct the inner forces of passion, desire, will, and intellect, is to be in possession of the destinies of men and nations.

As in ordinary science, there are, in this divine science, degrees of attainment; and a man is great in knowledge, great in himself, and great in his influence on the world, in the measure that he is great in self-control. He who understands and dominates the forces of external nature is the natural scientist; but be who understands and dominates the internal forces of the mind is the divine scientist; and the laws which operate in gaining a knowledge of external appearances, operate also in gaining a knowledge of internal varieties.

A man cannot become an accomplished scientist in a few weeks or months, nay, not even in a few years. But only after many years of painstaking investigation can he speak with authority, and be ranked among the masters of science. Likewise, a man cannot acquire self-control, and become possessed of the wisdom and peace giving knowledge which that self- control confers, but by many years of patient labor; a labor which is all the more arduous because it is silent, and both unrecognized and unappreciated by others; and he who would pursue this science successfully must learn to stand alone, and to toil unrewarded, as far as any outward emolument is concerned.

The natural scientist pursues, in acquiring his particular kind of knowledge, the following five orderly and sequential steps:

1. Observation: that is, he closely and persistently observes the facts of nature.

2. Experiment: Having become acquainted, by repeated observations, with certain facts, he experiments with those facts, with a view to the discovery of natural laws. He puts his facts through rigid processes of analysis, and so finds out what is useless and what of value; and he rejects the former and retains the latter.

3. Classification: Having accumulated and verified a mass of facts by numberless observations and experiments, he commences to classify those facts, to arrange them in orderly groups with the object of discovering some underlying law, some hidden and unifying principle, which governs, regulates, and binds together these facts.

4. Deduction: Thus he passes on to the fourth step of deduction. From the facts and results which are before him, he discovers certain invariable modes of action, and thus reveals the hidden laws of things.

5. Knowledge: Having proven and established certain laws, it may be said of such a man that he knows. He is a scientist, a man of knowledge.

But the attainment of scientific knowledge is not the end, great as it is. Men do not attain knowledge for themselves alone, nor to keep it locked secretly in their hearts, like a beautiful jewel in a dark chest. The end of such knowledge is use, service, the increase of the comfort and happiness of the world.

Thus, when a man has become a scientist, he gives the world the benefit of his knowledge, and unselfishly bestows upon mankind the results of all his labors. Thus, beyond knowledge, there is a further step of Use: that is, the right and unselfish use of the knowledge acquired; the application of knowledge to invention for the common weal.

It will be noted that the five steps or processes enumerated follow in orderly succession, and that no man can become a scientist who omits any one of them. Without the first step of systematic observation, for instance, he could not even enter the realm of knowledge of nature's secrets.

At first, the searcher for such knowledge has before him a universe of things: these things he does not understand; many of them, indeed, seem to be irreconcilably opposed one to the other, and there is apparent confusion; but by patiently and laboriously pursuing these five processes, he discovers the order, nature, and essences of things; perceives the central law or laws which bind them together in harmonious relationship, and so puts an end to confusion and ignorance. As with the natural scientist, so with the divine scientist; he must pursue, with the same self-sacrificing diligence, five progressive steps in the attainment of self-knowledge, self-control.

These five steps are the same as with the natural scientist, but the process is reversed, the mind, instead of being centered upon external things, is turned back upon itself, and the investigations are pursued in the realm of mind (of one's own mind) instead of in that of matter.

At first, the searcher for divine knowledge is confronted with that mass of desires, passions, emotions, ideas, and intellections which he calls himself, which is the basis of all his actions, and from which his life proceeds. This combination of invisible, yet powerful, forces appears confusedly; some of them stand, apparently, in direct conflict with each other, without any appearance or hope of reconciliation; his mind in its entirety, too, with his life which proceeds from that mind, does not seem to have any equitable relation to many other minds and lives about him, and altogether there is a condition of pain and confusion from which he would fain escape.

Thus, he begins by keenly realizing his state of ignorance, for no one could acquire either natural or divine knowledge, if he were convinced that without study or labor he already possessed it. With such perception of one's ignorance, there comes the desire for knowledge, and the novice in self-control enters upon the ascending pathway, in which are the following five steps:

1. Introspection. This coincides with the observation of the natural scientist. The mental eye is turned like a searchlight upon the inner things of the mind, and its subtle and ever varying processes are observed and carefully noted. This stepping aside from selfish gratifications, from the excitements of worldly pleasures and ambitions, in order to observe, with the object of understanding, one's nature, is the beginning of self-control. Hitherto, the man has been blindly and impotently borne along by the impulses of his nature, the mere creature of things and circumstances, but now he puts a check upon his impulses and, instead of being controlled, begins to control.

2. Self-analysis. Having observed the tendencies of the mind, they are then closely examined, and are put through a rigid process of analysis. The evil tendencies (those that produce painful effects) are separated from the good tendencies (those that produce peaceful effects); and the various tendencies, with the particular actions they produce, and the definite results which invariably spring from these actions, are gradually grasped by the understanding, which is at last enabled to

follow them in their swift and subtle interplay and profound ramifications. It is a process of testing and proving, and, for the searcher, a period of being tested and proved.

3. Adjustment. By this time, the practical student of things divine has clearly before him every tendency and aspect of his nature, down to the profoundest promptings of his mind, and the most subtle motives of his heart. There is not a spot or corner left, which he has not explored and illuminated with the light of self-examination. He is familiar with every weak and selfish point, every strong and virtuous quality. It is considered the height of wisdom to be able to see ourselves as others see us, but the practitioner of self-control goes far beyond this: he not only sees himself as others see him, he sees himself as he is. Thus, standing face to face with himself, not striving to hide away from any secret fault; no longer defending himself with pleasant flatteries; neither underrating nor overrating himself or his powers, and no more cursed with self-praise or self-pity, he sees the full magnitude of the task which lies before him; sees dearly ahead the heights of self-control, and knows

what work he has to do to reach them. He is no longer in a state of confusion, but has gained a glimpse of the laws which operate in the world of thought, and he now begins to adjust his mind in accordance with those laws. This is a process of weeding, sifting, cleansing. As the farmer weeds, cleans, and prepares the ground for his crops, so the student removes the weeds of evil from his mind, cleanses and purifies it preparatory to sowing the seeds of righteous actions which shall produce the harvest of a well ordered life.

4. Righteousness. Having adjusted his thoughts and deeds to those minor laws which operate in mental activities in the production of pain and pleasure, unrest and peace, sorrow and bliss, he now perceives that there is involved in those laws one Great Central Law which, like the law of gravitation in the natural world, is supreme in the world of mind; a law to which all thoughts and deeds are subservient, and by which they are regulated and kept in their proper sphere. This is the law of Justice or Righteousness, which is universal and supreme. To this law he now conforms. Instead of thinking and acting blindly, as the nature is stimulated

and appealed to by outward things, he subordinates his thoughts and deeds to this central principle. He no longer acts from self, but does what is right - what is universally and eternally right. He is no longer the abject slave of his nature and circumstances, he is the master of his nature and circumstances. He is no longer carried hither and thither on the forces of his mind; be controls and guides those forces to the accomplishment of his purposes. Thus, having his nature in control and subjection, not thinking thoughts nor doing deeds which oppose the righteous law, and which, therefore, that law annuls with suffering and defeat, he rises above the dominion of sin and sorrow, ignorance and doubt, and is strong, calm, and peaceful.

5. Pure Knowledge. By thinking right and acting right, he proves, by experience, the existence of the divine law on which the mind is framed, and which is the guiding and unifying principle in all human affairs and events, whether individual or national. Thus, by perfecting himself in self-control, he acquires divine knowledge; he reaches the point where it may be said of him, as of the natural scientist, that he knows. He has

mastered the science of self-control, and has brought knowledge out of ignorance, order out of confusion. He has acquired that knowledge of self which includes knowledge of all men; that knowledge of one's own life which embraces knowledge of all lives - for all minds are the same in essence (differing only in degree), are framed upon the same law; and the same thoughts and acts, by whatsoever individual they are wrought, will always produce the same results.

But this divine and peace bestowing knowledge, as in the case of the natural scientist, is not gained for one's self alone; for if this were so, the aim of evolution would be frustrated, and it is not in the nature of things to fall short of ripening and accomplishment; and, indeed, he who thought to gain this knowledge solely for his own happiness would most surely fail. So, beyond the fifth step of Pure Knowledge, there is a still further one of Wisdom, which is the right application of the knowledge acquired; the pouring out upon the world, unselfishly and without stint, the result of one's labors, thus accelerating progress and uplifting humanity.

It may be said of men who have not gone back into their own nature to control and purify it, that they cannot clearly distinguish between good and evil, right and wrong. They reach after those things which they think will give them pleasure, and try to avoid those things which they believe will cause them pain.

The source of their actions is self, and they only discover right painfully and in a fragmentary way, by periodically passing through severe sufferings, and lashings of conscience. But he who practices self-control, passing through the five processes, which are five stages of growth, gains that knowledge which enables him to act from the moral law which sustains the universe. He knows good and evil, right and wrong, and, thus knowing them, lives in accordance with good and right. He no longer needs to consider what is pleasant or what is unpleasant, but does what is right; his nature is in harmony with his conscience, and there is no remorse; his mind is in unison with the Great Law, and there is no more suffering and sin; for him evil is ended, and good is all in all.

3
Cause and Effect in Human Conduct

"All things, whether visible or invisible, are subservient to, and fall within the scope of, this infinite and eternal law of causation"

IT IS an axiom with the scientists that every effect is related to a cause. Apply this to the realm of human conduct, and there is revealed the principle of Justice. Every scientist knows (and now all men believe) that perfect harmony prevails throughout every portion of the physical universe, from the speck of dust to the greatest sun.

Everywhere there is exquisite adjustment. In the sidereal universe, with its millions of suns rolling majestically through space and carrying with them their respective systems of revolving planets, its vast nebula, its seas of meteors, and its vast army of comets traveling through illimitable space with inconceivable velocity, perfect order prevails; and again, in the natural world, with its multitudinous aspects of life, and its infinite variety of forms, there are the clearly defined limits of specific laws, through the operation of which all confusion is avoided, and unity and harmony eternally obtain. If this universal harmony could be arbitrarily broken, even in one small particular, the universe would cease to be; there could be no cosmos, but only universal chaos.

Nor can it be possible in such a universe of law that there should exist any personal power which is above, outside, and superior to, such law in the sense that it can defy it, or set it aside; for whatsoever beings exist, whether they be men or gods, they exist by virtue of such law; and the highest, best, and wisest among all beings would manifest his greater wisdom by his more complete obedience to that law which is wiser than wisdom, and than which nothing more perfect could be devised.

All things, whether visible or invisible, are subservient to, and fall within the scope of, this infinite and eternal law of causation. As all things seen obey it, so all things unseen - the thoughts and deeds of men, whether secret or open cannot escape it.

"Do right, it recompenseth; do one wrong – the equal retribution must be made." Perfect justice upholds the universe; perfect justice regulates human life and conduct. All the varying conditions of life, as they obtain in the world today, are the result of this law reacting on human conduct. Man can (and does) choose what causes he shall set in operation, but he cannot change the nature of effects; he can decide what thoughts he shall think, and what deeds he shall do, but he has no power over the results of those thoughts and deeds; these are regulated by the overruling law. Man has all power to act, but his power ends with the act committed. The result of the act cannot be altered, annulled, or escaped; it is irrevocable.

Evil thoughts and deeds produce conditions of suffering; good thoughts and deeds determine conditions of blessedness. Thus man's power is limited to, and his blessedness or misery is determined by his own conduct. To know this truth, renders life simple, plain, and unmistakable; all the crooked paths are straightened out, the heights of wisdom are revealed, and the open door to salvation from evil and suffering is perceived and entered.

Life may be likened to a sum in arithmetic. It is bewilderingly difficult and complex to the pupil who has not yet grasped the key to its correct solution, but once this is perceived and laid hold of, it becomes as astonishingly simple as it was formerly profoundly perplexing.

Some idea of this relative simplicity and complexity of life may be grasped by fully recognizing and realizing the fact that, while there are scores, and perhaps hundreds, of ways in which a sum may be done wrong, there is only one way by which it can be done right, and that when that right way is found the pupil knows it to be the right, his perplexity vanishes, and he knows that be has mastered the problem.

It is true that the pupil, while doing his sum incorrectly, may (and frequently does) think he has done it correctly, but he is not sure; his perplexity is still there, and if he is an earnest and apt pupil, he will recognize his own error when it is pointed out by the teacher.

So in life, men may think they are living rightly while they are continuing, through ignorance, to live wrongly; but the presence of doubt, perplexity, and unhappiness are sure indications that the right way has not yet been found. There are foolish and careless pupils who would like to pass a sum as correct before they have acquired a true knowledge of figures, but the eye and skill of the teacher quickly detect and expose the fallacy.

So in life there can be no falsifying of results; the eye of the Great Law reveals and exposes. Twice five will make ten to all eternity, and no amount of ignorance, stupidity, or delusion can bring the result up to eleven. If one looks superficially at a piece of cloth, he sees it as a piece of cloth, but if he goes further and inquires into its manufacture, and examines it closely and attentively, he sees that it is composed of a combination of individual threads, and that, while all the threads are interdependent, each thread pursues its own way throughout, never becoming confused with its sister thread. It is this entire absence of confusion between the particular threads which constitutes the finished work - a piece of cloth: any inharmonious commingling of the thread would result in a bundle of waste or a useless rag.

Life is like a piece of cloth, and the threads of which it is composed are individual lives. The threads, while being interdependent, are not confounded one with the other. Each follows its own course. Each individual suffers and enjoys the consequences of his own deeds, and not of the deeds of another. The course of each is simple and definite; the whole forming a complicated, yet harmonious, combination of sequences.

There are action and reaction, deed and consequence, cause and effect, and the counterbalancing reaction, consequence, and effect is always in exact ratio with the initiatory impulse. A durable and satisfactory piece of cloth cannot be made from shoddy material, and the threads of selfish thoughts and bad deeds will not produce a useful and beautiful life - a life that will wear well, and bear close inspection.

Each man makes or mars his own life; it is not made or marred by his neighbor, or by anything external to himself. Each thought he thinks, each deed he does, is another thread - shoddy or genuine - woven into the garment of his life; and as he makes the garment so must he wear it. He is not responsible for his neighbor's deeds; he is not the custodian of his neighbor's actions; he is responsible only for his own deeds; he is the custodian of his own actions.

The "problem of evil" subsists in a man's own evil deeds, and it is solved when those deeds are purified. Says Rosseau: "Man, seek no longer the origin of evil; thou thyself art its origin." Effect can never be divorced from cause; it can never be of a different nature from cause. Emerson says: "Justice is not postponed; a perfect equity adjusts the balance in all parts of life."

And there is a profound sense in which cause and effect are simultaneous, and form one perfect whole. Thus, upon the instant that a man thinks, say, a cruel thought, or does a cruel deed, that same instant he has injured his own mind; he is not the same man he was the previous instant; he is a little viler and a little more unhappy; and a number of such successive thoughts and deeds would produce a cruel and wretched man.

The same thing applies to the contrary - the thinking of a kind thought, or doing a kind deed - an immediate nobility and happiness attend it; the man is better than he was before, and a number of such deeds would produce a great and blissful soul.

Thus individual human conduct determines, by the faultless law of cause and effect, individual merit or demerit, individual greatness or meanness, individual happiness or wretchedness. What a man thinks, that he does; what he does, that he is. If be is perplexed, unhappy, restless, or wretched, let him look to himself, for there and nowhere else is the source of all his trouble.

4
Training of the Will

"Fixedness of purpose is at the root of all successful efforts, whether in things worldly or spiritual"

WITHOUT strength of mind, nothing worthy of accomplishment can be done, and the cultivation of that steadfastness and stability of character which is commonly called "willpower" is one of the foremost duties of man, for its possession is essentially necessary both to his temporal and eternal well being.

Fixedness of purpose is at the root of all successful efforts, whether in things worldly or spiritual, and without it man cannot be otherwise than wretched, and dependent upon others for that support which should be found within himself. The mystery which has been thrown around the subject of cultivation of the will by those who advertise to sell "occult advice" on the matter for so many dollars, should be avoided and dispelled, for nothing could be further removed from secrecy and mystery than the practical methods by which alone strength of will can be developed.

The true path of will cultivation is only to be found in the common everyday life of the individual, and so obvious and simple is it that the majority, looking for something complicated and mysterious, pass it by unnoticed.

A little logical thought will soon convince a man that he cannot be both weak and strong at the same time, that he cannot develop a stronger will while remaining a slave to weak indulgences, and that, therefore, the direct and only way to that greater strength is to assail and conquer his weaknesses.

All the means for the cultivation of the will are already at hand in the mind and life of the individual; they reside in the weak side of his character, by attacking and vanquishing which the necessary strength of will be developed. He who has succeeded in grasping this simple, preliminary truth, will perceive that the whole science of will cultivation is embodied in the following seven rules:

1. Break off bad habits.
2. Form good habits.
3. Give scrupulous attention to the duty of the present moment.
4. Do vigorously, and at once, whatever has to be done.
5. Live by rule.
6. Control the tongue.
7. Control the mind.

Anyone who earnestly meditates upon, and diligently practices, the above rules, will not fail to develop that purity of purpose and power of will which will enable him to successfully cope with every difficulty, and pass triumphantly through every emergency.

It will be seen that the first step is the breaking away from bad habits. This is no easy task. It demands the putting forth of great efforts, or a succession of efforts, and it is by such efforts that the will can alone be invigorated and fortified. If one refuses to take the first step, he cannot increase in willpower, for by submitting to a bad habit, because of the immediate pleasure which it affords, one forfeits the right to rule over himself, and is so far a weak slave.

He who thus avoids self-discipline, and looks about for some "occult secrets" for gaining willpower at the expenditure of little or no effort on his part, is deluding himself, and is weakening the willpower which he already possesses.

The increased strength of will which is gained by success in overcoming bad habits enables one to initiate good habits; for, while the conquering of a bad habit requires merely strength of purpose, the forming of a new one necessitates the intelligent direction of purpose.

To do this, a man must be mentally active and energetic, and must keep a constant watch upon himself. As a man succeeds in perfecting himself in the second rule, it will not be very difficult for him to observe the third, that of giving scrupulous attention to the duty of the present moment.

Thoroughness is a step in the development of the will which cannot be passed over. Slipshod work is an indication of weakness. Perfection should be aimed at, even in the smallest task. By not dividing the mind, but giving the whole attention to each separate task as it presents itself, singleness of purpose and intense concentration of mind are gradually gained - two mental powers which give weight and worth of character, and bring repose and joy to their possessor.

The fourth rule - that of doing vigorously, and at once, whatever has to be done - is equally important. Idleness and a strong will cannot go together, and procrastination is a total barrier to the acquisition of purposeful action. Nothing should be "put off" until another time, not even for a few minutes. That which ought to be done now should be done now.

This seems a little thing, but it is of far reaching importance. It leads to strength, success, and peace. The man who is to manifest a cultivated will must also live by certain fixed rules. He must not blindly gratify his passions and impulses, but must school them to obedience. He should live according to principle, and not according to passion. He should decide what he will eat and drink and wear, and what he will not eat and drink and wear; how many meals per day he will have, and at what times he will have them; at what time he will go to bed, and at what time get up. He should make rules for the right government of his conduct in every department of his life, and should religiously adhere to them.

To live loosely and indiscriminately, eating and drinking and sensually indulging at the beck and call of appetite and inclination, is to be a mere animal, and not a man with will and reason. The beast in man must be scourged and disciplined and brought into subjection, and this can only be done by training the mind and life on certain fixed rules of right conduct.

The saint attains to holiness by not violating his vows, and the man who lives according to good and fixed rules, is strong to accomplish his purpose.

The sixth rule, that of controlling the tongue, must be practiced until one has perfect command of his speech, so that he utters nothing in peevishness, anger, irritability, or with evil intent.

The man of strong will does not allow his tongue to run thoughtlessly and without check. All these six rules, if faithfully practiced, will lead up to the seventh, which is the most important of them all - namely, rightly controlling the mind.

Self-control is the most essential thing in life, yet least understood; but he who patiently practices the rules herein laid down, bringing them into requisition in all his ways and undertakings, will learn, by his own experience and efforts, how to control and train his mind, and to earn thereby the supreme crown of manhood - the crown of a perfectly poised will.

5

Thoroughness

"He who lacks thoroughness in his worldly duties, will also lack the same quality in spiritual things"

THOROUGHNESS consists in doing little things as though they were the greatest things in the world. That the little things of life are of primary importance, is a truth not generally understood, and the thought that little things can be neglected, thrown aside, or slurred over, is at the root of that lack of thoroughness which is so common, and which results in imperfect work and unhappy lives.

When one understands that the great things of the world and of life consist of a combination of small things, and that without this aggregation of small things the great things would be nonexistent, then he begins to pay careful attention to those things which he formerly regarded as insignificant. He thus acquires the quality of thoroughness, and becomes a man of usefulness and influence; for the possession or non-possession of this one quality may mean all the difference between a life of peace and power, and one of misery and weakness.

Every employer of labor knows how comparatively rare this quality is - how difficult it is to find men and women who will put thought and energy into their work, and do it completely and satisfactorily. Bad workmanship abounds. Skill and excellence are acquired by few. Thoughtlessness, carelessness, and laziness are such common vices that it should cease to appear strange that, in spite of "social reform," the ranks of the unemployed should continue to swell, for those who scamp their work today will, another day, in the hour of deep necessity, look and ask for work in vain.

The law of the survival of the fittest is not based on cruelty, it is based on justice: it is one aspect of that divine equity which everywhere prevails. Vice is "beaten with many stripes"; if it were not so, how could virtue be developed? The thoughtless and lazy cannot take precedence of, or stand equally with, the thoughtful and industrious.

A friend of mine tells me that his father gave all his children the following piece of advice: "Whatever your future work may be, put your whole mind upon it and do it thoroughly; you need then have no fear as to your welfare, for there are so many who are careless and negligent that the services of the thorough man are always in demand."

I know those who have, for years, tried almost in vain to secure competent workmanship in spheres which do not require exceptional skill, but which call chiefly for forethought, energy, and conscientious care. They have discharged one after another for negligence, laziness, incompetence, and persistent breaches of duty - not to mention other vices which have no bearing on this subject; yet the vast army of the unemployed continues to cry out against the laws, against society, and against Heaven.

The cause of this common lack of thoroughness is not far to seek; it lies in that thirst for pleasure which not only creates a distaste for steady labor, but renders one incapable of doing the best work, and of properly fulfilling one's duty.

A short time ago, a case came under my observation (one of many such), of a poor woman who was given, at her earnest appeal, a responsible and lucrative position. She had been at her post only a few days when she began to talk of the "pleasure trips" she was going to have now she had come to that place. She was discharged at the end of a month for negligence and incompetence.

As two objects cannot occupy the same space at the same time, so the mind that is occupied with pleasure cannot also be concentrated upon the perfect performance of duty. Pleasure has its own place and time, but its consideration should not be allowed to enter the mind during those hours which should be devoted to duty.

Those who, while engaged in their worldly task, are continually dwelling upon anticipated pleasures, cannot do otherwise than bungle through their work, or even neglect it when their pleasure seems to be at stake.

Thoroughness is completeness, perfection; it means doing a thing so well that there is nothing left to be desired; it means doing one's work, if not better than anyone else can do it, at least not worse than the best that others do. It means the exercise of much thought, the putting forth of great energy, the persistent application of the mind to its task, the cultivation of patience, perseverance, and a high sense of duty.

An ancient teacher said, "If anything has to be done, let a man do it, let him attack it vigorously"; and another teacher said, "Whatsoever thy hand findeth to do, do it with thy might."

He who lacks thoroughness in his worldly duties, will also lack the same quality in spiritual things. He will not improve his character; will be weak and half-hearted in his religion, and will not accomplish any good and useful end. The man who keeps one eye on worldly pleasure and the other on religion, and who thinks he can have the advantage of both conditions, will not be thorough either in his pleasure seeking or his religion, but will make a sorry business of both. It is better to be a whole-souled worldling than a half- hearted religionist; better to give the entire mind to a lower thing than half of it to a higher. It is preferable to be thorough, even if it be in a bad or selfish direction, rather than inefficient and squeamish in good directions, for thoroughness leads more rapidly to the development of character and the acquisition of wisdom; it accelerates progress and unfoldment; and while it leads the bad to something better, it spurs the good to higher and ever higher heights of usefulness and power.

6
Mind-Building and Life-Building

"Character is built in the same way as a tree or a house is built - namely, by the ceaseless addition of new material, and that material is thought."

EVERYTHING, both in nature and the works of man, is produced by a process of building. The rock is built up of atoms; the plant, the animal, and man are built up of cells; a house is built of bricks, and a book is built of letters.

A world is composed of a large number of forms, and a city of a large number of houses. The arts, sciences, and institutions of a nation are built up by the efforts of individuals. The history of a nation is the building of its deeds. The process of building necessitates the alternate process of breaking down. Old forms that have served their purpose are broken up, and the material of which they are composed enters into new combinations. There is reciprocal integration and disintegration. In all compounded bodies, old cells are ceaselessly being broken up, and new cells are formed to take their place.

The works of man also require to be continually renewed until they have become old and useless, when they are torn down in order that some better purpose may be served. These two processes of breaking down and building up in Nature are called death and life; in the artificial works of man they are called destruction and restoration. This dual process, which obtains universally in things visible, also obtains universally in things invisible. As a body is built of cells, and a house of bricks, so a man's mind is built of thoughts.

The various characters of men are none other than compounds of thoughts of varying combinations. Herein we see the deep truth of the saying, "As a man thinketh in his heart, so is he." Individual characteristics are fixed processes of thought; that is, they are fixed in the sense that they have become such an integral part of the character that they can be only altered or removed by a protracted effort of the will, and by much self-discipline.

Character is built in the same way as a tree or a house is built - namely, by the ceaseless addition of new material, and that material is thought. By the aid of millions of bricks a city is built; by the aid of millions of thoughts a mind, a character, is built. Every man is a mind builder, whether he recognizes it or not. Every man must perforce think, and every thought is another brick laid down in the edifice of mind. Such "brick laying" is done loosely and carelessly by a vast number of people, the result being unstable and tottering characters that are ready to go down under the first little gust of trouble or temptation.

Some, also, put into the building of their minds large numbers of impure thoughts; these are so many rotten bricks that crumble away as fast as they are put in, leaving always an unfinished and unsightly building, and one which can afford no comfort and no shelter for its possessor.

Debilitating thoughts about one's health, enervating thoughts concerning unlawful pleasures, weakening thoughts of failure, and sickly thoughts of self-pity and self-praise are useless bricks with which no substantial mind temple can be raised.

Pure thoughts, wisely chosen and well placed, are so many durable bricks which will never crumble away, and from which a finished and beautiful building, and one which affords comfort and shelter for its possessor, can be rapidly erected.

Bracing thoughts of strength, of confidence, of duty; inspiring thoughts of a large, free, unfettered, and unselfish life, are useful bricks with which a substantial mind temple can be raised; and the building of such a temple necessitates that old and useless habits of thought be broken down and destroyed. "Build thee more stately mansions, Oh my soul! As the swift seasons roll."

Each man is the builder of himself. If he is the occupant of a jerry-built hovel of a mind that lets in the rains of many troubles, and through which blow the keen winds of oft recurring disappointments, let him get to work to build a more noble mansion which will afford him better protection against those mental elements.

Trying to weakly shift the responsibility for his jerry-building on to the devil, or his forefathers, or anything or anybody but himself, will neither add to his comfort, nor help him to build a better habitation.

When he wakes up to a sense of his responsibility, and an approximate estimate of his power, then he will commence to build like a true workman, and will produce a symmetrical and finished character that will endure, and be cherished by posterity, and which, while affording a never failing protection for himself, will continue to give shelter to many a struggling one when he has passed away.

The whole visible universe is framed on a few mathematical principles. All the wonderful works of man in the material world have been brought about by the rigid observance of a few underlying principles; and all that there is to the making of a successful, happy, and beautiful life, is the knowledge and application of a few simple, root principles.

If a man is to erect a building that is to resist the fiercest storms, he must build it on a simple, mathematical principle, or law, such as the square or the circle; if he ignores this, his edifice will topple down even before it is finished.

Likewise, if a man is to build up a successful, strong, and exemplary life - a life that will stoutly resist the fiercest storms of adversity and temptation - it must be framed on a few simple, undeviating moral principles.

Four of these principles are Justice, Rectitude, Sincerity, and Kindness. These four ethical truths are to the making of a life what the four lines of a square are to the building of a house.

If a man ignores them and thinks to obtain success and happiness and peace by injustice, trickery, and selfishness, he is in the position of a builder who imagines he can build a strong and durable habitation while ignoring the relative arrangement of mathematical lines, and he will, in the end, obtain only disappointment and failure.

He may, for a time, make money, which will delude him into believing that injustice and dishonesty pay well; but in reality his life is so weak and unstable that it is ready at any moment to fall; and when a critical period comes, as come it must, his affairs, his reputation, and his riches crumble to ruins, and he is buried in his own desolation. It is totally impossible for a man to achieve a truly successful and happy life who ignores the four moral principles enumerated, whilst the man who scrupulously observes them in all his dealings can no more fail of success and blessedness than the earth can fail of the light and warmth of the sun so long as it keeps to its lawful orbit; for he is working in harmony with the fundamental laws of the universe; he is building his life on a basis which cannot be altered or overthrown, and, therefore, all that he does will be so strong and durable, and all the parts of his life will be so coherent, harmonious, and firmly knit that it cannot possibly be brought to ruin.

In all the universal forms which are built up by the Great Invisible and unerring Power, it will be found that the observance of mathematical law is carried out with unfailing exactitude down to the most minute detail. The microscope reveals the fact that the infinitely small is as perfect as the infinitely great. A snowflake is as perfect as a star. Likewise, in the erection of a building by man, the strictest attention must be paid to every detail.

A foundation must first be laid, and, although it is to be buried and hidden, it must receive the greatest care, and be made stronger than any other part of the building; then stone upon stone, brick upon brick is carefully laid with the aid of the plumb line, until at last the building stands complete in its durability, strength, and beauty.

Even so it is with the life of a man. He who would have a life secure and blessed, a life freed from the miseries and failures to which so many fall victims, must carry the practice of the moral principles into every detail of his life, into every momentary duty and trivial transaction.

In every little thing he need be thorough and honest, neglecting nothing. To neglect or misapply any little detail - be he commercial man, agriculturist, professional man, or artisan - is the same as neglecting a stone or a brick in a building, and it will be a source of weakness and trouble.

The majority of those who fail and come to grief do so through neglecting the apparently insignificant details. It is a common error to suppose that little things can be passed by, and that the greater things are more important, and should receive all attention; but a cursory glance at the universe, as well as a little serious reflection on life, will teach the lesson that nothing great can exist which is not made up of small details, and in the composition of which every detail is perfect.

He who adopts the four ethical principles as the law and base of his life, who raises the edifice of character upon them, who in his thoughts and words and actions does not wander from them, whose every duty and every passing transaction is performed in strict accordance with their exactions, such a man, laying down the hidden foundation of integrity of heart securely and strongly, cannot fail to raise up a structure which shall bring him honor; and he is building a temple in which he can repose in peace and blessedness - even the strong and beautiful Temple of his life.

7
Cultivation and Concentration

"Every successful man, in whatever direction his success may lie, practices concentration"

CONCENTRATION, or the bringing of the mind to a center and keeping it there, is vitally necessary to the accomplishment of any task. It is the father of thoroughness and the mother of excellence. As a faculty, it is not an end in itself, but is an aid to all faculties, all work. Not a purpose in itself, it is yet a power which serves all purposes.

Like steam in mechanics, it is a dynamic force in the machinery of the mind and the functions of life. The faculty is a common possession, though in its perfection it is rare - just as will and reason are common possessions, though a perfectly poised will and a comprehensive reason are rare possessions - and the mystery which some modern mystical writers have thrown around it is entirely superfluous.

Every successful man, in whatever direction his success may lie, practices concentration, though he may know nothing about it as a subject of study; every time one becomes absorbed in a book or task, or is rapt in devotion or assiduous in duty, concentration, in a greater or lesser degree, is brought into play.

Many books purporting to give instructions on concentration make its practice and acquisition an end in itself. Than this, there is no surer nor swifter way to its destruction. The fixing of the eyes upon the tip of the nose, upon a doorknob, a picture, a mystical symbol, or the portrait of a saint; or the centering of the mind upon the navel, the pineal gland, or some imaginary point in space (I have seen all these methods seriously advised in works on this subject) with the object of acquiring concentration, is like trying to nourish the body by merely moving the jaw as in the act of eating, without taking food. Such methods prevent the end at which they aim. They lead towards dispersion and not concentration; towards weakness and imbecility rather than towards power and intelligence.

I have met those who have squandered, by these practices, what measure of concentration they at first possessed, and have become the prey of a weak and wandering mind. Concentration is an aid to the doing of something; it is not the doing of something in itself. A ladder has no divine knowledge, or the sweeping of a floor - without resorting to methods which have no practical bearing on life; for what is concentration but the bringing of a well controlled mind to the doing of that which has to be done? He who does his work in an aimless, a hurried, or thoughtless manner, and resorts to his artificial "concentration methods" - to his doorknob, his picture, or nasal extremity in order to gain that which he imagines to be some kind of mystical power - but which is a very ordinary and practical quality - though he may drift towards insanity (and I knew one man who became insane by these practices), he will not increase in steadiness of mind.

The great enemy of concentration - and therefore of all skill and power - is a wavering, wandering, undisciplined value in and of itself, but only in so far as it enables us to reach something which we could not otherwise reach.

In like manner, concentration is that which enables the mind to accomplish with ease that which it would be otherwise impossible to accomplish; but of itself it is a dead thing, and not a living accomplishment.

Concentration is so interwoven with the uses of life that it cannot be separated from duty; and he who tries to acquire it apart from his task, his duty, will not only fail, but will diminish, and not increase, his mental control and executive capacity, and so render himself less and less fit to succeed in his undertakings.

A scattered and undisciplined army would be useless. To make it effective in action and swift in victory it must be solidly concentrated and masterfully directed. Scattered and diffused thoughts are weak and worthless. Thoughts marshaled, commanded, and directed upon a given point, are invincible; confusion, doubt, and difficulty give way before their masterly approach.

Concentrated thought enters largely into all successes, and informs all victories. There is no more secret about its acquirement than about any other acquisition, for it is governed by the underlying principle of all development, namely, practice. To be able to do a thing, you must begin to do it, and keep on doing it until the thing is mastered.

This principle prevails universally - in all arts, sciences, trades; in all learning, conduct, religion. To be able to paint, one must paint; to know how to use a tool skillfully, he must use the tool; to become learned, he must learn; to become wise, he must do wise things; and to successfully concentrate his mind, he must concentrate it.

But the doing is not all - it must be done with energy and intelligence. The beginning of concentration, then, is to go to your daily task and put your mind on it, bringing all your intelligence and mental energy to a focus upon that which has to be done; and every time the thoughts are found wandering aimlessly away, they should be brought promptly back to the thing in hand.

Thus the "center" upon which you are to bring your mind to a point, is (not your pineal gland or a paint in space), but the work which you are doing every day; and your object in thus concentrating is to be able to do your work with smooth rapidity and consummate skill; for until you can thus do your work, you have not gained any degree of control over the mind; you have not acquired the power of concentration.

This powerful focusing of one's thought and energy and will upon the doing of things is difficult at first - as everything worth acquiring is difficult - but daily efforts, strenuously made and patiently followed up, will soon lead to such a measure of self-control as will enable one to bring a strong and penetrating mind to bear upon any work undertaken; a mind that will quickly comprehend all the details of the work, and dispose of them with accuracy and dispatch.

He will thus, as his concentration capacity increases, enlarge his usefulness in the scheme of things, and increase his value to the world, thus inviting nobler opportunities, and opening the door to higher duties; he will also experience the joy of a wider and fuller life.

In the process of concentration there are the four following stages:

1. Attention.

2. Contemplation.

3. Abstraction.

4. Activity in Repose.

At first the thoughts are arrested, and the mind is fixed upon the object of concentration, which is the task in hand - this is attention. The mind is then roused into vigorous thought concerning the way of proceeding with the task - this is contemplation. Protracted contemplation leads to a condition of mind in which the doors of the senses are all closed against the entrance of outside distractions, the thoughts being wrapped in, and solely and intensely centered upon, the work in hand - this is abstraction.

The mind thus centered in profound cogitation reaches a state in which the maximum of work is accomplished with the minimum of friction - this is activity in repose. Attention is the first stage in all successful work. They who lack it fail in everything. Such are the lazy, the thoughtless, the indifferent and incompetent.

When attention is followed by an awakening of the mind to serious thought, then the second stage is reached. To ensure success in all ordinary, worldly undertakings, it is not necessary to go beyond these two stages. They are reached, in a greater or lesser degree, by all that large army of skilled and competent workers which carries out the work of the world in its manifold departments, and only a comparatively small number reach the third stage of abstraction; for when abstraction is reached, we have entered the sphere of genius.

In the first two stages, the work and the mind are separate, and the work is done more or less laboriously, and with a degree of friction; but in the third stage, a marriage of the work with the mind takes place, there is a fusion, a union, and the two become one: then there is a superior efficiency with less labor and friction.

In the perfection of the first two stages, the mind is objectively engaged, and is easily drawn from its center by external sights and sounds; but when the mind has attained perfection in abstraction, the subjective method of working is accomplished, as distinguished from the objective.

The thinker is then oblivious to the outside world, but is vividly alive in his mental operations. If spoken to, he will not hear; and if plied with more vigorous appeals, he will bring back his mind to outside things as one coming out of a dream; indeed, this abstraction is a kind of waking dream, but its similarity to a dream ends with the subjective state: it does not obtain in the mental operations of that state, in which, instead of the confusion of dreaming, there is perfect order, penetrating insight, and a wide range of comprehension.

Whoever attains to perfection in abstraction will manifest genius in the particular work upon which his mind is centered. Inventors, artists, poets, scientists, philosophers, and all men of genius, are men of abstraction. They accomplish subjectively, and with ease, that which the objective workers - men who have not yet attained beyond the second stage in concentration - cannot accomplish with the most strenuous labor.

When the fourth stage - that of activity in repose - is attained, then concentration in its perfection is acquired. I am unable to find a single word which will fully express this dual condition of intense activity combined with steadiness, or rest, and have therefore employed the term "activity in repose."

The term appears contradictory, but the simple illustration of a spinning top will serve to explain the paradox. When a top spins at the maximum velocity, the friction is reduced to the minimum, and the top assumes that condition of perfect repose which is a sight so beautiful to the eye, and so captivating to the mind, of the schoolboy, who then says his top is "asleep." The top is apparently motionless, but it is the rest, not of inertia, but of intense and perfectly balanced activity.

So the mind that has acquired perfect concentration is, when engaged in that intense activity of thought which results in productive work of the highest kind, in a state of quiet poise and calm repose. Externally, there is no apparent activity, no disturbance, and the face of a man who has acquired this power will assume a more or less radiant calmness, and the face will be more sublimely calm when the mind is most intensely engaged in active thought.

Each stage of concentration has its particular power. Thus the first stage, when perfected, leads to usefulness; the second leads to skill, ability, talent; the third leads to originality and genius; while the fourth leads to mastery and power, and makes leaders and teachers of men. In the development of concentration, also, as in all objects of growth, the following stages embody the preceding ones in their entirety.

Thus in contemplation, attention is contained; in abstraction, both attention and contemplation are embodied; and he who has reached the last stage, brings into play, in the act of contemplation, all the four stages. He who has perfected himself in concentration is able, at any moment, to bring his thoughts to a point upon any matter, and to search into it with the strong light of an active comprehension. He can both take a thing up and lay it down with equal deliberation. He has learned how to use his thinking faculties to fixed purposes, and guide them towards definite ends. He is an intelligent doer of things, and not a weak wanderer amid chaotic thought.

Decision, energy, alertness, as well as deliberation, judgment, and gravity, accompany the habit of concentration; and that vigorous mental training which its cultivation involves, leads, through ever increasing usefulness and success in worldly occupations, towards that higher form of concentration called "meditation," in which the mind becomes divinely illumined, and acquires the heavenly knowledge.

8
Practice of Meditation

"By concentration a man may acquire the wonderful comprehension and vast power of a Caesar; by meditation he may reach the divine wisdom and perfect peace of a Buddha"

When aspiration is united to concentration, the result is meditation. When a man intensely desires to reach and realize a higher, purer, and more radiant life than the merely worldly and pleasure loving life, he engages in aspiration; and when he earnestly concentrates his thoughts upon the finding of that life, be practices meditation.

Without intense aspiration, there can be no meditation. Lethargy and indifference are fatal to its practice. The more intense the nature of a man, the more readily will he find meditation, and the more successfully will he practice it. A fiery nature will most rapidly scale the heights of Truth in meditation, when its aspirations have become sufficiently awakened. Concentration is necessary to worldly success: meditation is necessary to spiritual success. Worldly skill and knowledge are acquired by concentration: spiritual skill and knowledge are acquired by meditation.

By concentration a man can scale the highest heights of genius, but he cannot scale the heavenly heights of Truth: to accomplish this, he must meditate. By concentration a man may acquire the wonderful comprehension and vast power of a Caesar; by meditation he may reach the divine wisdom and perfect peace of a Buddha.

The perfection of concentration is power; the perfection of meditation is wisdom. By concentration, men acquire skill in the doing of the things of life - in science, art, trade, etc, - but by meditation, they acquire skill in life itself, in right living, enlightenment, wisdom, etc.

Saints, sages, saviors, wise men and divine teachers - are the finished products of holy meditation. The four stages in concentration are brought into play in meditation; the difference between the two powers being one of direction, and not of nature.

Meditation is therefore spiritual concentration; the bringing of the mind to a focus in its search for the divine knowledge, the divine life; the intense dwelling, in thought, on Truth. Thus a man aspires to know and realize, above all things else, the Truth; he then gives attention to conduct, to life, to self-purification: giving attention to these things, he passes into serious contemplation of the facts, problems, and mystery of life: thus contemplating, he comes to love Truth so fully and intensely as to become wholly absorbed in it, the mind is drawn away from its wanderings in a multitude of desires, and, solving one by one the problems of life, realizes that profound union with Truth which is the state of abstraction; and thus absorbed in Truth, there is that balance and poise of character, that divine action in repose, which is the abiding calm and peace of an emancipated and enlightened mind.

Meditation is more difficult to practice than concentration because it involves a much more severe self-discipline than that which obtains in concentration.

A man can practice concentration without purifying his heart and life, whereas the process of purification is inseparable from meditation. The object of meditation is divine enlightenment, the attainment of Truth, and is therefore interwoven with practical purity and righteousness.

Thus while, at first, the time spent in actual meditation is short - perhaps only half an hour in the early morning - the knowledge gained in that half hour of vivid aspiration and concentrated thought is embodied in practice during the whole day.

In meditation, therefore, the entire life of a man is involved; and as he advances in its practice he becomes more and more fitted to perform the duties of life in the circumstances in which he may be placed, for he becomes stronger, holier, calmer, and wiser. The principle of meditation is twofold, namely:

1. Purification of the heart by repetitive thought on pure things.
2. Attainment of divine knowledge by embodying such purity in practical life.

Man is a thought being, and his life and character are determined by the thoughts in which he habitually dwells. By practice, association, and habit, thoughts tend to repeat themselves with greater and greater ease and frequency; and so "fix" the character in a given direction by producing that automatic action which is called "habit."

By daily dwelling upon pure thoughts, the man of meditation forms the habit of pure and enlightened thinking which leads to pure and enlightened actions and well performed duties. By the ceaseless repetition of pure thoughts, he at last becomes one with those thoughts, and is a purified being, manifesting his attainment in pure actions, in a serene and wise life.

The majority of men live in a series of conflicting desires, passions, emotions, and speculations, and there are restlessness, uncertainty, and sorrow; but when a man begins to train his mind in meditation, he gradually gains control over this inward conflict by bringing his thoughts to a focus upon a central principle.

In this way the old habits of impure and erroneous thought and action are broken up, and the new habits of pure and enlightened thought and action are formed; the man becomes more and more reconciled to Truth, and there is increasing harmony and insight, a growing perfection and peace. A powerful and lofty aspiration towards Truth is always accompanied with a keen sense of the sorrow and brevity and mystery of life, and until this condition of mind is reached, meditation is impossible.

Merely musing, or whiling away the time in idle dreaming (habits to which the word meditation is frequently applied), are very far removed from meditation, in the lofty spiritual sense which we attach to that condition. It is easy to mistake reverie for meditation. This is a fatal error which must be avoided by one striving to meditate. The two must not be confounded.

Reverie is a loose dreaming into which a man falls; meditation is a strong, purposeful thinking into which a man rises. Reverie is easy and pleasurable; meditation is at first difficult and irksome. Reverie thrives in indolence and luxury; meditation arises from strenuousness and discipline. Reverie is first alluring, then sensuous, and then sensual.

Meditation is first forbidding, then profitable, and then peaceful. Reverie is dangerous; it undermines self-control. Meditation is protective; it establishes self-control.

There are certain signs by which one can know whether he is engaging in reverie or meditation. The indications of reverie are:

1. A desire to avoid exertion.
2. A desire to experience the pleasures of dreaming.
3. An increasing distaste for one's worldly duties.
4. A desire to shirk one's worldly responsibilities.
5. Fear of consequences.
6. A wish to get money with as little effort as possible.
7. Lack of self-control.

The indications of meditation are:

1. Increase of both physical and mental energy.

2. A strenuous striving after wisdom.

3. A decrease of irksomeness in the performance of duty.

4. A fixed determination to faithfully fulfill all worldly responsibilities.

5. Freedom from fear.

6. Indifference to riches.

7. Possession of self-control.

There are certain times, places, and conditions in and under which it is impossible to meditate, others wherein it is difficult to meditate, and others wherein meditation is rendered more accessible; and these, which should be known and carefully observed, are as follows: Times, Places, and Conditions in which Meditation is Impossible:

1. At, or immediately after, meals.

2. In places of pleasure.

3. In crowded places.

4. While walking rapidly.

5. While lying in bed in the morning.

6. While smoking.

7. While lying on a couch or bed for physical or mental relaxation.

Times, Places and Conditions in which Meditation is Difficult:

1. At night.

2. In a luxuriously furnished room.

3. While sitting on a soft, yielding seat.

4. While wearing gay clothing.

5. When in company.

6. When the body is weary.

7. If the body is given too much food.

Times, Places, and Conditions in which it is best to Meditate:

1. Very early in the morning.

2. Immediately before meals.

3. In solitude.

4. In the open air or in a plainly furnished room.

5. While sitting on a hard seat.

6. When the body is strong and vigorous.

7. When the body is modestly and plainly clothed.

It will be seen by the foregoing instructions that ease, luxury, and indulgence (which induce reverie) render meditation difficult, and when strongly pronounced make it impossible; while strenuousness, discipline, and self- denial (which dispel reverie), make meditation comparatively easy.

The body, too, should be neither overfed nor starved; neither in rags nor flauntingly clothed. It should not be tired, but should be at its highest point of energy and strength, as the holding of the mind to a concentrated train of subtle and lofty thought requires a high degree of both physical and mental energy.

Aspiration can often best be aroused, and the mind renewed in meditation, by the mental repetition of a lofty precept, a beautiful sentence or a verse of poetry. Indeed, the mind that is ready for meditation will instinctively adopt this practice.

Mere mechanical repetition is worthless, and even a hindrance. The words repeated must be so applicable to one's own condition that they are dwelt upon lovingly and with concentrated devotion. In this way aspiration and concentration harmoniously combine to produce, without undue strain, the state of meditation.

All the conditions above stated are of the utmost importance in the early stages of meditation, and should be carefully noted and duly observed by all who are striving to acquire the practice; and those who faithfully follow the instructions, and who strive and persevere, will not fail to gather in, in due season, the harvest of purity, wisdom, bliss, and peace; and will surely eat of the sweet fruits of holy meditation.

9

The Power of Purpose

"Purpose is the keystone in the temple of achievement. It binds and holds together in a complete whole that which would otherwise he scattered and useless"

DISPERSION is weakness; concentration is power. Destruction is a scattering, preservation a uniting, process. Things are useful and thoughts are powerful in the measure that their parts are strongly and intelligently concentrated.

Purpose is highly concentrated thought. All the mental energies are directed to the attainment of an object, and obstacles which intervene between the thinker and the object are, one after another, broken down and overcome.

Purpose is the keystone in the temple of achievement. It binds and holds together in a complete whole that which would otherwise he scattered and useless. Empty whims, ephemeral fancies, vague desires, and half-hearted resolutions have no place in purpose. In the sustained determination to accomplish there is an invincible power which swallows up all inferior considerations, and marches direct to victory.

All successful men are men of purpose. They hold fast to an idea, a project, a plan, and will not let it go; they cherish it, brood upon it, tend and develop it; and when assailed by difficulties, they refuse to be beguiled into surrender; indeed, the intensity of the purpose increases with the growing magnitude of the obstacles encountered. The men who have molded the destinies of humanity have been men mighty of purpose.

Like the Roman laying his road, they have followed along a well defined path, and have refused to swerve aside even when torture and death confronted them.

The Great Leaders of the race are the mental road makers, and mankind follows in the intellectual and spiritual paths which they have carved out and beaten. Great is the power of purpose. To know how great, let a man study it in the lives of those whose influence has shaped the ends of nations and directed the destinies of the world.

In an Alexander, a Caesar, or a Napoleon, we see the power of purpose when it is directed in worldly and personal channels; in a Confucius, a Buddha, or a Christ, we perceive its vaster power when its course is along heavenly and impersonal paths. Purpose goes with intelligence.

There are lesser and greater purposes according with degrees of intelligence. A great mind will always be great of purpose. A weak intelligence will be without purpose. A drifting mind argues a measure of undevelopment.

What can resist an unshakable purpose? What can stand against it or turn it aside? Inert matter yields to a living force, and circumstance succumbs to the power of purpose. Truly, the man of unlawful purpose will, in achieving his ends, destroy himself, but the man of good and lawful purpose cannot fail. It only needs that he daily renew the fire and energy of his fixed resolve, to consummate his object.

The weak man, who grieves because be is misunderstood, will not greatly achieve; the vain man, who steps aside from his resolve in order to please others and gain their approbation, will not highly achieve; the double minded man, who thinks to compromise his purpose, will fail.

The man of fixed purpose who, whether misunderstandings and foul accusations, or flatteries and fair promises, rain upon him, does not yield a fraction of his resolve, is the man of excellence and achievement; of success, greatness, power.

Hindrances stimulate the man of purpose; difficulties nerve him to renewed exertion; mistakes, losses, pains, do not subdue him; and failures are steps in the ladder of success, for be is ever conscious of the certainty of final achievement. All things at last yield to the silent, irresistible, all conquering energy of purpose.

"Out of the night that covers me, Black as the pit from pole to pole, I thank whatever gods may be For my unconquerable soul. In the fell clutch of circumstance I have not whined nor cried aloud; Under the bludgeoning of chance My head is bloody but unbowed. It matters not how strait the gate, How charged with punishment the scroll; I am the master of my fate, I am the captain of my soul."

10

The Joy of Accomplishment

"Blessed is the man who strives against his own selfishness; he will taste in its fullness the joy of accomplishment."

JOY IS ALWAYS the accompaniment of a task successfully accomplished. An undertaking completed, or a piece of work done, always brings rest and satisfaction. "When a man has done his duty, he is light-hearted and happy," says Emerson; and no matter how insignificant the task may appear, the doing of it faithfully and with whole-souled energy always results in cheerfulness and peace of mind.

Of all miserable men, the shirker is the most miserable. Thinking to find ease and happiness in avoiding difficult duties and necessary tasks, which require the expenditure of labor and exertion, his mind is always uneasy and disturbed, he becomes burdened with an inward sense of shame, and forfeits manliness and self-respect.

"He who will not work according to his faculty, let him perish according to his necessity," says Carlyle; and it is a moral law that the man who avoids duty, and does not work to the full extent of his capacity, does actually perish, first in his character and last in his body and circumstances.

Life and action are synonymous, and immediately a man tries to escape exertion, either physical or mental, he has commenced to decay. On the other hand, the energetic increase in life by the full exercise of their powers, by overcoming difficulties, and by bringing to completion tasks which coiled for the strenuous use of mind or muscle.

How happy is a child when a school lesson, long labored over, is mastered at last!

The athlete, who has trained his body through long months or years of discipline and strain, is richly blessed in his increased health and strength; and is met with the rejoicings of his friends when he carries home the prize from the field of contest.

After many years of ungrudging toil, the heart of the scholar is gladdened with the advantages and powers which learning bestows.

The business man, grappling incessantly with difficulties and drawbacks, is amply repaid in the happy assurance of well earned success; and the horticulturist, vigorously contending with the stubborn soil, sits down at last to eat of the fruits of his labor.

Every successful accomplishment, even in worldly things, is repaid with its own measure of joy; and in spiritual things, the joy which supervenes upon the perfection of purpose is sure, deep and abiding. Great is the heartfelt joy (albeit ineffable) when, after innumerable and apparently unsuccessful attempts, some ingrained fault of character is at last cast out to trouble its erstwhile victim and the world no more.

The striver after virtue - he who is engaged in the holy task of building up a noble character - tastes, at every step of conquest over self, a joy which does not again leave him, but which becomes an integral part of his spiritual nature.

All life is a struggle; both without and within there are conditions against which man must contend; his very existence is a series of efforts and accomplishments, and his right to remain among men as a useful unit of humanity depends upon the measure of his capacity for wrestling successfully with the elements of nature without, or with the enemies of virtue and truth within.

It is demanded of man that he shall continue to strive after better things, after greater perfection, after higher and still higher achievements; and in accordance with the measure of his obedience to this demand, does the angel of joy wait upon his footsteps and minister unto him; for he who is anxious to learn, eager to know, and who puts forth efforts to accomplish, finds the joy which eternally sings at the heart of the universe.

First in little things, then in greater, and then in greater still, must man strive; until at last be is prepared to make the supreme effort, and strive for the accomplishment of Truth, succeeding in which, he will realize the eternal joy.

The price of life is effort; the acme of effort is accomplishment; the reward of accomplishment is joy.

Blessed is the man who strives against his own selfishness; he will taste in its fullness the joy of accomplishment.

THE END

Master of Destiny

Master of Destiny

Printed in Great Britain
by Amazon